Happy 75th, Dad!
Love,
   Joan and Walt

DELTA COUNTRY

NARRATIVE
Richard Dillon

PHOTOGRAPHS
Steve Simmons

FOREWORD
Harold Gilliam

DELTA COUNTRY

For
DR. GEORGE P. HAMMOND
Bancroft Library

Published by Presidio Press, 31 Pamaron Way, Novato, CA 94947.
Library of Congress Cataloging in Publication Data. Dillon, Richard H. Delta country. Bibliography: p. Include index. 1. Delta Region (Calif.)—History.
2. Delta Region (Calif.)—Description and travel. I. Simmons, Steve. II. Title. F868.D45D54   979.4'24   82-7546   ISBN: 0-89141-147-X   AACR2
Jacket design, Kathleen A. Jaeger. Book design, Lyn Cordell. Composition, Helen Epperson. Cartography, Bill Yenne. Printed in the United States of America.

PRESIDIO PRESS

Contents

MANY PEOPLE HAVE HELPED, BUT PARTICULAR
THANKS GO TO:

Steve Simmons
Joan Griffin
Dr. John Thompson
Dr. David Lantis
Dr. Richard Logan
Frank Almeda
Ray Brian
Stephen W. Hastings and the National Maritime
     Museum
Louis Stein
Richard Terry and the California State Library
Elliott Castello
Ferol Egan
Gary Kurutz
Eleanor Capelle, Frank Glover, and the Sutro Library
Peter Evans and the Forestry Library, University of
     California, Berkeley
Harold Gilliam
Irene Moran and the Bancroft Library
David Myrick
Barbara Brooks Schoenwald
Ralph Moreno and the Mill Valley Public Library
Dr. James Thorpe White and Jennie Darsie White
Henry Schact

Acknowledgments

BEFORE THE BIG STIR OVER THE PERIPHERAL Canal, which began in the late 1970s, if you mentioned "the Delta" to most Californians they probably would have conjured up visions of New Orleans paddlewheel steamboats and banjos strumming in the moonlight. Except for a relatively few boat owners, duck hunters, and fishermen, few people realized that California had a delta of its own. This region of land and water was terra incognita, the state's ultima Thule.

If this Delta were almost anywhere but California —in the Midwest, for example—it would no doubt have been heralded as a major scenic wonder and perhaps would be protected as a national park. But as Richard Dillon notes here, the Delta's islands, winding channels, and austere marshland beauty have historically been overlooked by writers and travelers enraptured by the state's more flamboyant landscapes.

Consequently, when the Peripheral Canal debate focused attention here, Californians curious about the Delta could find very little information on it. Richard Dillon in this book admirably makes it possible to fill in this blank space on our mental maps of the state.

The Delta is not only California's least-known scenic and recreational attraction, with a rich history of its own, it is an invaluable resource in at least three other ways—as fabulously rich farmland, as a central water source for a dry region, and as a complex ecosystem whose influence extends far beyond its own margins.

In Gold Rush days the Delta was a huge swamp where the waters of the five-hundred-mile Central

Foreword

Valley and surrounding mountains came together in a tangle of braided channels and sloughs. For thousands of years the matted reeds and tules and mosses had grown and decayed, season by season, until they formed ever-increasing layers of peat—decomposed plant matter—in some places as deep as fifty feet.

The agricultural story of the Delta began on the day some unknown settler discovered beneath the tules the deep beds of fertile peat soil. Men who had built sluices on the streams of the Mother Lode began to build levees in the Delta, and along the drained edges and islands of the great marsh, tules were replaced by wheat. Gradually the Delta became a maze of river channels and diked islands that produced record bounties of such crops as potatoes and asparagus for America's dinner tables.

But the Delta has been the source of an even greater bounty: fresh water. Eight rivers draining California's interior flow into the main trunk streams—the Sacramento from the north and the San Joaquin from the south—which converge here in the Delta's thousand miles of winding waterways before flowing west to merge with the salt waters of San Francisco Bay. The Delta is an immense natural reservoir whose waters have long been coveted by agriculturists and developers in the arid southern part of the state.

In the years after World War II, the federal government built a giant pumping plant on the Delta's southwestern edge, near Tracy, as part of the Central Valley Project. The pumps lifted water two hundred feet and sent it flowing south by gravity through the Delta-Mendota Canal to irrigate the rich soils of the San Joaquin Valley. Two decades later, the state of California tapped the Delta in the same area and built a parallel aqueduct, the California Canal, extending much farther south, ultimately to another series of pumps drawing the water over the Tehachapi Mountains into the Los Angeles basin. En route the canal supplied water to irrigate the San Joaquin's west side.

Besides being a vital element of California's agriculture and a central reservoir for its waters, the Delta is also a diverse ecosystem supporting immense populations of fish and wildlife. Migratory birds by the hundreds of thousands spend the winter here or stop over on their seasonal flights of thousands of miles. In the fall, when the lakes of Alaska and Canada begin to freeze over, great flocks of ducks come down the Pacific Flyway—pintails and mallards and cinnamon teals and widgeons. Long-billed curlews probe the pasturelands, and skeins of geese appear against the gray winter sky. Knowledgeable bird-watchers know where to find colonies of rare sandhill cranes and whistling swans.

Even greater populations of aquatic species have their habitats in the channels. The silvery schools of king salmon that once entered the Golden Gate and migrated through the Delta to spawn in the headwaters of tributary streams have dwindled greatly since the construction of dams on most of the rivers, but, partly owing to hatcheries on the rivers, there are still substantial salmon runs in spring, fall, and winter. The most abundant game fish in the Delta is the striped bass, which was introduced from the Atlantic Coast a century ago and proliferated until sport fishermen were hauling in more than one million annually. The stripers winter in the central Delta and move upstream in the spring to spawn. Also transplanted from the Atlantic were the shad, which migrate from the ocean through the Delta in the spring and swim as far as they can go up the tributary rivers and streams.

The biggest creature in the Delta's waters is the sturgeon, a huge, horny-skinned fish with a head resembling that of a crocodile. One-hundred-pounders are common, and the largest weigh in at half a ton or more. Vital to the Delta's chain of life are the masses of aquatic organisms—including worms and other invertebrates—that furnish food for the birds and fish.

In recent years the sport fish populations have steadily declined owing to a number of causes, including increased water withdrawals which suck fish to the aqueduct intakes. As increasing quantities of the Delta's fresh water are consumed by the aqueducts, salt water moves into the channels from the Bay. The Delta's natural ecosystem, in which there are whole ranges of life corresponding to the various stages in the transition between saline water and fresh, is thrown out of balance.

If the withdrawals are substantially increased, salt water could come farther into the Delta, endangering not only the fish that depend on river flow but the irrigated farmlands, the birds that require fresh water, and the entire food chain. Salt water in the Delta could also seep into the deep aquifers that supply San Joaquin Valley wells far beyond the Delta itself.

Statisticians are fond of calculating the economic value of the agriculture, the fisheries, and the bird life that would be doomed by excessive withdrawals of fresh water. But the ultimate value of this haunting landscape and all of its varied forms of life cannot be tallied on a computer. It has something to do with the human place in nature's intricate patterns. Living in balance with the earth's biological systems is a matter of human survival. What we do to the Delta, we do to ourselves. As Richard Dillon and Steve Simmons eloquently demonstrate in these pages, this place is ours to enjoy—and to nurture.

Harold Gilliam

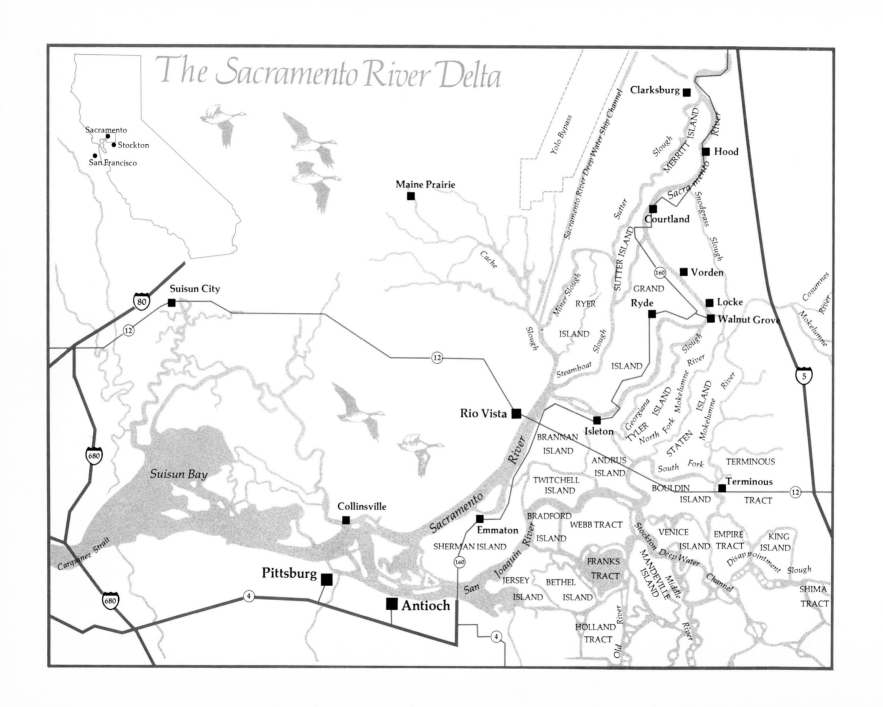

The Sacramento River Delta

Sacramento
Stockton
San Francisco

Clarksburg

Yolo Bypass

Sacramento River Deep Water Ship Channel

MERRITT ISLAND

Hood

Maine Prairie

Sutter Slough

Sacramento River

Snodgrass Slough

Courtland

SUTTER ISLAND

Cache

Vorden

160

GRAND

Ryde

Locke

Cosumnes River

Suisun City

80

12

RYER

ISLAND

Mine Slough

Slough

Walnut Grove

Slough

Mokelumne River

Mokelumne River

5

12

Steamboat

Slough

ISLAND

Slough

Georgiana Slough

TYLER ISLAND

North Fork

STATEN ISLAND

Mokelumne River

Rio Vista

River

Isleton

BRANNAN

ISLAND

ANDRUS

ISLAND

South Fork

TERMINUS

680

Suisun Bay

TWITCHELL

ISLAND

BOULDIN

ISLAND

Terminous

TRACT

12

Collinsville

BRADFORD

ISLAND

WEBB TRACT

VENICE

ISLAND

EMPIRE

TRACT

KING

ISLAND

Emmaton

Sacramento River

SHERMAN ISLAND

160

San Joaquin River

Stockton Deep Water

MANDEVILLE ISLAND

Channel

Disappointment Slough

SHIMA

TRACT

Carquinez Strait

Pittsburg

FRANKS

TRACT

Middle River

680

4

JERSEY

ISLAND

BETHEL

ISLAND

Antioch

San

Old River

HOLLAND

TRACT

4

THERE ARE MANY IMPRESSIVE DELTAS IN THE world, from Egypt's baking Nile to Russia's frigid Lena. But among all these floodplains, the Sacramento–San Joaquin River Delta is truly one of a kind.

Even in its natural state, before it was tamed by pioneering Californians, the area fifty-odd miles northeast of San Francisco was unique—a delta, a fen, and an estuary all rolled into one. A delta is defined as an alluvial fan through which a river enters a sea via two or more mouths. It is often triangular in shape like the Greek letter *delta* from which it takes its name. A delta is created by the accumulated deposit of sediments carried downstream by a "braided" river, one grown sluggish and twisting as terrain flattens. An estuary is a sea-drowned river mouth; the place where tides and currents meet to do battle at the expense of the traditional "innocent bystander," in this case the land itself. As for a fen, the word is simply Old English for marsh.

Early settlers discovered the extraordinary fertility of the Delta soil and began the never-ending job of holding back the waters. Swampland slowly became farmland. Now, after more than a hundred years of reclamation, this freshwater arm of San Francisco Bay has been transformed into an immense garden that also serves as an aquatic sports paradise.

The Delta, a broad flatland arteried by the pulsating Sacramento and San Joaquin rivers and veined by countless sluggish sloughs, has been noticed by many of the West's great travelers and writers—John C. Fremont, Mark Twain, John Muir, Mary Austin, and Jack London. (London did some of his writing on a

Part One
The Lay of the Land

houseboat, or "ark," drifting on Georgiana Slough.) But all were either hastening elsewhere or were so distracted by writing chores or other business that they failed to recognize the Delta's singular and alluring prospects. As a result, it has had no Thoreau, no Muir, to this day.

There is nothing spectacular or grand about the low-lying triangle by which California's Central Valley rivers seek the sea—except, at times, its sky. The skyscape can be a tremendous pile of billowing cumulus clouds, sometimes as dramatic as the firmament over the Arizona desert or the heavens off the Kona Coast. But the flattened horizon is broken only by the distant bulk of Mount Diablo's saddle. Spectacle is the business of our desert mesas and buttes; the jagged and surf-battered Redwood Coast; or the High Sierra, where the Sacramento and San Joaquin are born in springs, snowbanks, and even glaciers. The Delta, in contrast, is a bucolic land of peace, a tranquil place of ease largely unsullied by civilization. It is low-keyed; it must be approached on its own unhurried terms in order to be properly appreciated. It is a backwater, a throwback in a few hidden "gunkholes," or anchorages, to the pristine landscape of the Spanish explorers and, everywhere else, to the easygoing rural and pastoral California of a century ago. Time stands still. It is almost as much "an island in time" as Harold Gilliam's lonesome Point Reyes Peninsula.

No frantic Baedeker can catalog the region's attributes from speeding automobile or power cruiser. By land, the Delta is best seen *à la* shank's mare, by the hiker trudging along a levee crown at the infantryman's steady three miles per hour. On water, the real Delta is virtually invisible to the powerboat operator and the water-skier in tow. They are much too low down; from the water's surface they see nothing but the dikes that wall them in. They might just as well be whizzing down a blank canal. But a houseboat, pushed along at less than ten miles per hour by an outboard "kicker," falls into the rhythm of the Delta, and from the upper deck, the land beyond the levee tops becomes visible—the historic gardens, orchards, and grainfields of the area's geometric geography.

The Delta is really two worlds—one of water and leisure, the other of cropland and (intermittent) hard work. Strangely enough, while they are hardly symbiotic, they are compatible if, much of the time, oblivious of one another.

Legend to the contrary, most areas of the Delta can be approached by road as well as by waterway, though not always on pavement. Slow meandering along the narrow and shoulderless levee roads or even on the Delta's three main highways (4, 12, and 160) is a good way to see—and savor—the Delta, with frequent stops to absorb such local color as that of the little "Asparagus Capital of the World" (Isleton), or Locke, the West's only all-Chinese town. The highway traveler, if unhurried, can appreciate the subtle and graceful charm of the region, with its leisurely pace and relaxed lifestyle.

The traveler sees, first, the obvious—that the Delta is a mighty stage for a balancing act of nature between land and water, in which man-made dikes have given the land a temporary and precarious edge over the currents of the rolling rivers and the swell of the Pacific, whose compulsive tides reach even beyond the Delta. From the air, one becomes aware that the confusing maze, a geographical jigsaw puzzle seemingly designed for Paul Bunyan, sorts itself out into a bizarre archipelago of enormous islands, checkerboarded and patchworked by agricultural furrows. These are encircled by the narrow and twisting channels that make up the "water wonderland" of the pleasure boating fraternity. But it takes the dimension of time, not the differing viewpoints of land, water, and air, to feel the nostalgic sense of history and tradition underlying the surface features of dikes and bridges, marinas and barns.

Although the Delta has had, as yet, few chroniclers compared with the Sierra Nevada or the Mother Lode country, the region's charm is enhanced by an interesting past. Small wonder that its perceptive young photographer, Steve Simmons, writes, "A bit of history lies around every bend of the levee road, within every building, along every street."

To reach the historic heart of the Delta, it is only necessary to drive a few miles north from Antioch on Highway 160. The traveler will get some sense of the Delta's spell as he crosses Sherman, Brannan, and Andrus islands and passes through such sleepy, poignant old towns (once steamboat landings) as Isleton, Walnut Grove, Locke, Courtland, Hood, and Freeport, before the road terminates in Sacramento's urban sprawl. In scarcely fifty miles of leisurely driving, the visitor will see what Mary Austin called The Land of the

Little Duck. It is on the Pacific Flyway, so it is a land of mallards and teal, herons and egrets, geese and red-winged blackbirds, and especially, absurd coots, or mudhens. But Miss Austin was referring to California Indian mythology. It was Little Duck who tossed up the primordial mud of the Delta to make California's mountains.

But the Delta is not only interesting and scenic, it is important. It is the keystone of California's water supply, although it occupies only 1 percent of the state's land area. It is a fragile keystone. Just eleven hundred miles of channel-front levees prevent it from reverting to the swampy wilderness found by Spanish explorers.

A third of the entire state drains directly into the structurally depressed fault basin that is the great Central Valley, then out of this sagging geosyncline by way of the Delta. It must not be forgotten that urban-industrial, commercial, and technological California remains the leading agricultural state of the United States, with a gross of $15.5 billion annually. Agriculture, and thus the "health" of the Central Valley and Delta, is absolutely vital to the state's well-being. When agriculture is redefined as "agribusiness," it not only provides $40 billion a year to the state's economy but also furnishes jobs for 2.5 million Californians.

California's Delta is unlike the archetypal delta of the Mississippi, which pushes out to make an impressive bulge on the Louisiana shore of the Gulf of Mexico. The joint delta of California's two master streams makes no such offshore swelling. On the contrary, it narrows where a normal delta widens, at its seaward edge, and it is tucked more than thirty miles inland from the open sea. It forms an inner sanctum of an estuary that, to the west, swells into an inland sea, San Francisco Bay. Delta and bay were created at the same time, when the Coast Range was flooded by the sea at the end of the last ice age. You have to go thirty-five miles east of Carquinez Strait before you leave sea level entirely. The land then begins to rise six feet to the mile, and an elevation of about fifty feet rims the eastern edge of the great sea marsh.

The Sacramento River's gradient between the city of Sacramento and Rio Vista is only half a foot per mile compared to the cutting stream's seven feet per mile between Red Bluff and Redding. The lower river sprawls about awkwardly, seeking sea level by dividing itself into an interlacing network of channels and side channels. Some of the latter—sloughs—are water-filled only in winter and spring; some are dead ends. The channels of the river near its mouth are distributaries, the opposite of tributaries. They steal water and alluvium and carry them away from the main stream between natural, always rising, levees—the riverbanks. These are built up, like alluvial fans, by the stream's deposition of sediment.

Almost at its mouth, the 382-mile-long Sacramento River is joined by a major tributary, the San Joaquin River. The latter drains three-fifths of the Central Valley, the Sacramento the other two-fifths. But, for all of its length, 317 miles, the San Joaquin's flow and velocity cannot compare with the Sacramento's. The latter contributes 74 percent of the Delta's water, the San Joaquin only 21 percent. Several minor affluents add the remaining 5 percent.

California's two great watercourses merge at Sherman Island in a consternating maze of channels, sloughs, and islands, some of the latter eleven thousand acres in size. This is why the English navigator of 1837, Capt. Edward Belcher, called the Delta an archipelago and why nature writer Harold Gilliam calls its puzzle of isles and thousand-mile channels, even today, "an explorer's paradise."

The Sacramento, swollen with San Joaquin water at the very last moment, enters Suisun Bay, then passes through a narrow gash—Carquinez Strait—between the Mount Diablo Range and the Montezuma Hills. It enters San Pablo Bay and is then lost in the tides of San Francisco Bay as it seeks the sea by way of the Golden Gate.

The two streams that combine in the Delta compose one of the half-dozen largest river systems in this country and, easily, the biggest one within the confines of a single state. They drain sixty thousand square miles of interior valley, an area the size of all New England, carrying twenty million acre-feet of water annually through the precarious leveed channels of the Delta. This is enough *aqua pura* to serve a quarter of the state's land surface or 60 percent of its population for a year, or the city of San Francisco for two hundred years.

A Southern Pacific land promoter of circa 1910, A. J. Wells, estimated that there were 250,000 acres of Delta lands. He was much too conservative. Dr. John Thompson of the University of Illinois Geography Department, who knows the Delta better than anyone else, estimates that there are 565,000 acres of peat and alluvial land, about 56 percent of it below sea level and about 45,000 acres not land at all but standing water. Dr. David Lantis of Chico State University's Geography Department restricts the region to 490,000 acres, about 307,000 acres of it in peatland.

Geographers differ in their definition of the Delta. Dr. Thompson compares it to the fens of Great Britain. Travel and booster literature once likened the Delta portions of the counties of Sacramento, San Joaquin, Contra Costa, Solano, and Yolo not to England's fens but to the Zuider Zee, itself. The Delta was called America's Holland. A Benicia picture postcard publisher, Frank J. Stumm, used to issue views entitled "Beautiful Rio Vista, Calif., Capital of the American Netherlands."

Dr. Lantis admits that the swamped tule basin of the great river junction has many deltaic features, such as low-lying islands, distributaries, marshes, and stream banks grown into natural levees. But because it lacks one critical element of true deltas, the foreset layering of fresh deposition of alluvium, he is more comfortable calling it an interrupted delta. Dr. Richard Logan of UCLA considers the Sacramento–San Joaquin confluence to be a true delta because it satisfies the major criterion of the breed: the twin rivers deposit alluvium into standing water. This is called sublacustrine (under-lake) or submarine (undersea) deposition. The floodplains of much of the Central Valley, on the other hand, are floored by fans of alluvial material laid out subaerially, that is, on dry ground, not in standing water.

The triangle of the Delta has its rough apexes at Sacramento, Stockton, and Antioch. Sacramento is some ten miles beyond the Delta per se; but the capital is inextricably linked to the flooded tule basin by history, economics, and politics.

An idealized map of the Delta must take into account cultural or human factors as well as such purely geographical criteria as terrain and hydrography. It would be the most wiggly and out-of-shape "triangle" drafted since Euclid. Its western border would begin at either the east end of Carquinez Strait (Dr. Logan) or the east end of Suisun Bay (Dr. Thompson). The line would then run along the Antioch shore to dip southward to touch bottom at Banta and the nearby bridges that cross the San Joaquin River. From this point, the boundary would swing northward to French Camp and Stockton. From Stockton, the east side of the great triangle would run along a transition zone where floodplains give way to the reddening soil of the dry plains, the "prairies" of forty-niner Gold Rush accounts. This line, at the five- or ten-foot contour line, is well to the west of Lodi, Galt, and Elk Grove, but passes through Thornton and Hood to end its northward course at Clarksburg, below Freeport.

From a point west of Clarksburg the boundary, enclosing the Yolo Bypass and the Sacramento River Deep Water Ship Channel, would run southwest to Maine Prairie, then loop around the base of the Montezuma Hills via Rio Vista, Collinsville, and Birds Landing to Montezuma and Suisun sloughs. From Suisun City and Cordelia the Delta's edge drops due south to the starting point of Carquinez Strait.

Since, curiously, the Sacramento and San Joaquin share a combined valley, with no watershed dividing the two great arteries, it is necessary to pick an arbitrary point where one valley ends and the other begins. Over the years, experts have used the Mokelumne River or the Cosumnes River as the dividing line.

Cordelia, Suisun, and the steamboat-landing ghost town of Collinsville are the most westerly of Delta settlements. Rio Vista sits on higher ground at the base of the Montezuma Hills but it is Deltan by orientation and faces the mid-Delta across the Sacramento lapping at its feet. Towns in the very heart of the Delta, some of them hardly hamlets now, are Isleton, Ryde, Walnut Grove, Locke, Courtland, Clarksburg, Hood, and Terminous. Vorden and Paintersville are more sites now than settlements, and a few towns, like Emmaton, have vanished utterly.

If west-to-east Highway 12 across the Delta from Rio Vista to Lodi via Terminous is taken as a rough dividing line between the Sacramento Delta and that of the San Joaquin, many more square and wet miles of tracts; islands, channels, cuts, and sloughs lie south of the road. Yet most of the Delta's history, with the one great exception of Stockton, is north of that highway's white line. The interior towns have all grown up on the Sacramento, except French Camp and the city of Stockton. Sacramento outstripped the latter city, from the start, in its sociopolitical importance. It became the major terminal for post–Gold Rush steamboating from San Francisco. From it spread the first genuine settlers of the Delta, to homesteads and subsistence farms atop the high natural levees south of the city, not on the banks of the sunny San Joaquin. Finally, the great booms in pears, potatoes, and asparagus had their starts in the north, although all were forced, in time, to move San Joaquinward.

Since the 1850s, the Delta has been reclaimed, polderized. (In the Delta, the word tract is used in lieu of the European term *polder*.) By dikes and dams and ditches, its wet lowlands have been transformed into croplands. Today it is, agriculturally, among the richest areas of the world. It was the first to be reclaimed by efficient, innovative methods involving modern machinery. Clamshell dredges, steam traction engines, Holt "Caterpillar" tractors, LeTourneau earth-moving equipment, all had their start there.

The soil of much of the Delta is a rich peat, the residue of eons of deposition and decay of tules, or bulrushes. The earliest vegetation of the swampland was the common reed, *Phragmites australis (Cav.) Trin. ex Steud.* It was joined by some of California's one hundred varieties of sedge, by coarse grasses, and particularly by tules and California bulrushes. These the Spaniards lumped together as *tules*, and the Delta was *Los Tulares* or the singular *El Tular*, the Land of the Rush Beds. Early Americans confused the tules with cattails and dubbed them "flags." The tule was long known as *Scirpus lacustris L.* and sometimes as *Scirpus totora*, or simply *Scirpus spp.*, but the ubiquitous Delta rush is really *Scirpus acutus Muhl. ex Bigel.* The other common bulrush is *Scirpus californicus (C. A. Mey) Steud.*

The peat, a light, organic humus, has become

mixed with waterborne silt, or river muck, to become an altered soil. Much of the muck is a mineral soil with blue clay prominent in its makeup. The mixing was accelerated by hydraulic mining far off in the Mother Lode and, especially, the Northern Mines of the Sierra gold country. The resulting "slickens" swept downstream, sometimes taking barns, stock, and farmhouses with it, to become the Delta's "slum" which, quite literally, clogged up the Sacramento River as well as overlaying the tule muck beds. This alluvial fill is concentrated on the edges of the Delta. The heart of the watery basin is composed mostly of indigenous peaty fill, not alluvium.

The Delta's 300,000-plus acres of peatland average eighteen feet in thickness, deepening to fifty feet in the west and shallowing to only four feet toward the northern edge of the region, where mineral soil takes over. The latter, surprisingly, is more fertile than the dead plant matter, as well as being much less inclined to subsidence. The organic overlay is usually about three feet or less of decomposed tules atop the thick layer of ancient reeds, then a mineral substream of alluvial and lacustrine (that is, both stream- and lake-deposited) soft muck, and finally hardpan.

Compared to clay, peat soil is a shifty substitute for levee building. It compresses under weight, like kapok; in the Delta the load can be anything from a small herd of Herefords to the mass of a huge dike. It subsides, literally shrinks and sinks, due to oxidation as well as deflation. The average elevation of the depressed, saucerlike centers of drained peat islands ranges from five feet to ten feet *below* sea level. The problems of drainage and seepage are frightening, as islands sink while river bottoms rise from the accretion of silt. Peat soil is also so light that, when dry, it blows away in miniature dust storms. Besides this wind erosion problem, peat is also inflammable. But it is excellent for agriculture and ideal for intensive land use, well worth the enormous expense and long years of effort it has taken to reclaim the land.

In its original state, three-fifths of the Delta was awash at ordinary tides. High spring tides, especially when combined with westerly winds and high river run-off, submerged not only the islands but the huge back-swamps or flood basins. Local relief was very slight. The most prominent features were the asymmetrical natural levees or stream banks. When the Delta was turned into a sea by flooding, new "islands" appeared— sand hummocks, Indian mounds, the crests of the highest natural levees, and the tops of drowned trees. The natural levees on the west end of Sherman Island were so low, almost at the level of Suisun Bay at low tide, that they disappeared at high water. But upstream were higher natural levees on Staten, Grand, and Brannan islands, with large growths of trees.

Around Isleton, both high and broad banks appeared and at the junction of Steamboat Slough and the Sacramento they were four to six hundred feet wide. These natural levees or dikes were fourteen feet high at the heads of Grand and Sutter islands, twenty-four feet high near the city of Sacramento. The riverbanks had abrupt faces on the water, but they did not erode away, because of their covering of vegetation. Their back-slopes also dropped steeply inland. Often the distance from the crown of a natural levee to the island level was only fifty to a hundred yards. The next highest prereclamation features were lofty sand mounds around the San Joaquin's Old River and the towns of Knightsen and Oakley. Some towered seventeen feet above the surrounding swamps.

About 320,000 acres of the Delta comprised its original tidal basin, more than half disappearing under water at high tides. Another 205,000 acres were subject to river inundation but free of tidal flooding except at (rare) extreme high tides. A measure of the success of reclamation is the fact that this tidal area had shrunk by 1957 to barely 39,000 acres. Alluviation of channels and the rupturing of levees, some permanent as in (1938) Franks Tract, have kept this tidewater area from further shrinkage.

The Sacramento River peaks between January and May but can flood anywhere from mid-November to May. Snowmelt floods, however, are but a tenacious myth. Between 1910 and 1950, fifty-two winter rain floods struck the Sacramento River's basin, but not one came from snowmelt. The latter does damage only when combined with intense rainstorms on land already saturated by earlier precipitation.

The San Joaquin River peaks later in the year, from March to June. Winter rain crests are high and quick, the snow runoff water lower but longer-lasting. Since the flow is so much less than in the Sacramento, the San Joaquin does not seem to miss its lack of basins and floodways; it makes do with its limited bottomlands.

The San Joaquin's longest tributary, the Mokelumne River, also sees its peak flow in the spring and early summer. Its channel cuts only slightly into the floodplain before spreading out across a fan west of Woodbridge to enter the Delta. A typical mountain stream for seventy-five miles, the Mokelumne becomes confused, bewildered, at sea level. Geographers, till about 1866, did not know whether to call it a tributary to the Sacramento or to the San Joaquin, because it is connected to the former by sea level sloughs. Before reclamation at least, the river seemed to run uphill, feeding the Sacramento Basin to the north by way of Snodgrass Slough and (until it was closed) Tyler Slough.

Because of a lower alluvial fan than other streams and a high rate of erosion and deposition, the Mokelumne's current pushes a great burden of dirt down its channel, rather than simply spreading it on its fan. This deposit has actually deflected the Sacramento westward, though the river does manage to carry off a large part of this sediment. With its tributaries, the Cosumnes River and Dry Creek, the Mokelumne produces 2,642,000 acre-feet of water, or 22 percent of the entire runoff of the San Joaquin Valley.

The Cosumnes River drains a basin of 580 square miles. It discharges 880,000 acre-feet annually into the Mokelumne just before that stream's deltaic mouths debouch into the marshlands. Its indefinite course meanders aimlessly through several channels. The shifting bed of the Cosumnes has left behind abandoned channels and river bends as well as little lakes, sloughs, and marshy "tracts." But its high banks are inhabitable year-round.

Dry Creek is an intermittent arroyo draining 280 square miles, but discharging only 162,000 acre-feet of water by way of a wide and shallow bed. Tidal influences are felt in it, but during some summers, the stream is only a series of stagnant pools. The smallest tributary to the Mokelumne is tortuous Jahant Slough, a wide and shallow bed without a stream trench, that terminates in Tracy Lake, though it sometimes has connected with the Mokelumne.

The Calaveras is a real river, usually perennial, but sometimes it goes dry and fails to reach the San Joaquin at Stockton. This is because it is not a High Sierra stream like the Mokelumne, but rises only fifty miles from the Delta, in the foothills. It drains 490 square miles of 340,000 acre-feet. When it divides, the north fork remains the Calaveras, while the southern branch, though once the more important channel, becomes Mormon Slough. Historic French Camp Slough, to the south, carries water all year and probably connected with Mormon Slough in the distant past.

The mighty Sacramento's velocity is low in the Delta and it was lower yet before man-made dikes prevented its spreading into vast backswamps. But even slow-moving water can deluge the Delta. There were floods in 1805, 1825–26, and 1846–47, but there were virtually no improvements of any kind to destroy. The first well-documented flood was in the winter of 1849–50. It was followed by one in May–June, 1850, in which the Sacramento overflowed all the way from Freeport to Walnut Grove, overtopped Steamboat Slough's banks by two feet, and left only the berms of Indian mounds peeping above the surface. The spring of

1852 saw a three-month siege by floodwaters, which was repeated in the winter of 1852–53. After a brief ebb, it started all over again in April–June, 1853, causing the first real pressure on the legislature by Stocktonians for levee building.

From 1853 till 1861, almost in alternating years, natural banks and artificial levees gave way to runoff, tides, and wind-whipped waves. The worst floods were those of the winter of 1861–62, seemingly the greatest inundation anywhere since Noah cast off.

The floodwaters submerged the city of Sacramento and washed Rio Vista out to sea. They sent such a torrent down the Yolo Basin, out through Cache Slough, and back into the rambunctious Sacramento again, that its current was literally dammed by a wall of water. Besides checking the current, absurdly, in its own bed and in Steamboat Slough, this Yolo-bypassed Sacramento water then took advantage of the weak current in the San Joaquin and ran up that stream some distance before turning and joining the normal flow around French Camp. Next, the Sacramento swept a sheet of water across Twitchell, Brannan, and Andrus islands—they just disappeared—and temporarily merged the two rivers into just one stream. The latter quickly vanished into a dirty yellow sea three hundred miles long by twenty wide. Buildings floated off their foundations and were smashed to kindling in the roily waters. Many head of livestock were drowned before they could be picked up from high riverbanks and Indian mounds by steamers and scows hurriedly pressed into rescue service. The vast extent of flooding could easily be measured after the waters receded because Bermuda grass from a test patch near Sacramento was spread over hundreds of square miles of the Delta.

In Stockton, the alarm was sounded on the day after Christmas, 1861. By January, the city was under a foot of water and its citizens saw a freshwater sea stretching unbroken to the Coast Range. Just as it began to drain off, the untamed Sacramento replenished it. Water at the head of Roberts Island rose to twelve feet above the normal winter's low tide level. Ten miles north of Rio Vista, water in Lindsey Slough stood at an incredible eighteen and a half feet above low tide level. Rowboat regattas were popular in Sacramento's suddenly Venetian streets. The legislature, like Norway rats, fled an apparently sinking Capitol, to reconvene in San Francisco. The floodwaters reached almost to Georgetown, now Franklin; Isaac ("Uncle Isaac") F. Freeman told historian W. J. Davis that the plains east of the river were covered with stock, dead or dying in the mud and dirty water. An opportunist named Meany made much money by killing mired cattle and stealing their hides.

There was little or no letup after the disaster of 1861–62. In 1867–68 the Yolo Basin and Maine Prairie were swamped. In 1871 it was the turn of the Calaveras River; in 1873, Jersey Island; in 1874, Bouldin Island and the Bethel Tract, the old Sand Mound Ranch. In 1875, Sherman Island's levees were breached by tides, and Twitchell Island's levee was moved inland by hydrostatic pressure. That same winter, floods overtopped dikes on the San Joaquin River, Rough and Ready Island, and Reclamation District 17. When the San Joaquin's Old River became choked with driftwood and sand, the water, naturally, struck out in search of low ground. It dodged the man-made levees of upper Roberts Island, raced through Paradise Cut, and swamped the Byron Tract.

Perhaps to celebrate the Centennial Year, nature gave the Delta a breather in 1876. Only little Marsh Creek went over its banks, wetting the reclaimed area south of Jersey Island.

But Mother Nature was only summoning her strength. A gopher-riddled levee collapsed in February, 1878 with an angry roar and, in the usual domino action, filled the Yolo Basin to overflowing, then washed away lower river dikes and the village of Emmaton on Sherman Island. (Residents anchored their houses like arks to the crown of the levee and tried to wait out the flood on upper floors. But they were uprooted and shipwrecked.) Freeport, Clarksburg, and Walker Landing were half drowned, and parts of Isleton set sail. The Delta suffered $10 million in damage, the worst of it on Grand, Brannan, and Andrus islands.

A follow-up flood in May ignored the already sodden Sacramento Basin and vented its fury on the San Joaquin. Union Island just up and disappeared beneath the waves. Roberts Island and District 17 on the mainland survived, though only knolls rose, like islands, above the water. Much grain and livestock were lost. Some students of the Delta believe that the 1878 floods were so drastic that they wiped out the native fauna, allowing its replacement by such exotics as pheasants and muskrats.

In 1879 it was not flooding but seepage that vexed the farmers by destroying some Mokelumne River crops. But floods reoccurred in 1886, 1890, and 1893, then almost every year from 1899 to 1912. After a strange but welcome respite, they resumed in 1928, 1936, 1938, 1940, and 1950. Franks Tract was first overwhelmed in 1936, but its levees were repaired. In 1938 it was so badly drowned that its farmers abandoned it forever to fishermen and yachtsmen. During that same 1938 waterstorm, a dredge hurrying to save Venice Island nearly capsized, and Quimby Island's levee, weakened by beaver tunnels, gave way.

December of 1955 saw the Yuba City disaster, whose effects were also felt on the lower Sacramento. In Franklin and in the capital, skiffs once more took to the streets. Worse for the Stone Lake area of the Sacramento flood basin near Hood was the spring flood of 1958. Much of Elliott Castello's cattle ranch was submerged, and for the first time in memory, stock had to be moved out of boggy areas.

In 1972, Isleton was isolated, cut off from the world. In 1980 a levee breached before wave action, flooding Upper and Lower Jones Tract. Only an obstinate railroad embankment saved the area from a worse disaster.

Flooding has been the main problem in the Delta, but there is also the threat of salinization. Salt water usually stops a few miles above Antioch. (Circa 1900, the C & H sugar refinery at Crockett used to draw fresh water directly from Carquinez Strait, but this is no longer possible.) The Sacramento's tidal waters are not normally saline, though tides can be felt all the way up to Verona, at the junction of the Feather with the Sacramento 130 miles from the Golden Gate. Exceptions occur only in very late summers or autumns of drought years with little runoff. Suisun Bay is still "sweet" in winter and spring, becoming brackish in mid-July. The early Spaniards named the bay *Puerto Dulce*, or "Sweet" (i.e., "Fresh") Port. The Hudson's Bay Company trappers in the Delta in the 1830s called it Freshwater Bay.

Salting has not yet permanently impaired reclamation and there has been, as yet, no need to flush newly reclaimed land with fresh water. Nor has there been evidence of salt damage, so far, to cropland after summertime levee breaks.

At times, however, Delta water becomes too brackish to drink, or even to put to farm use. This was the case in the Antioch area in 1841, and again in the 1860s and 1870s. In the seventies, Twitchell Island residents had to go upstream to the Mokelumne to find potable water. From about 1911 to 1925, there were no real floods, so salinization increased. In a few of the Delta's so-called Critical Years (1920, 1924, 1926, 1931, 1934, and 1939), the water was unfit even for irrigation. The very worst years, 1924 and 1931, brought serious crop losses from salinity. Farmers were forced to haul in water for both domestic and livestock use. The 1931 drought saw two-thirds of the Delta's channels grow salty. Late that summer, and in the fall, the Sacramento River barely kept pace with evaporation and no fresh water reached San Francisco Bay. Since the controlled release of water from Shasta Dam after 1945, this has not recurred. But only the pressure of a constant flow in the Sacramento is a barrier to saltwater invasion of the Delta.

Since the diversion of Central Valley water above the Delta to urban use and irrigation, saltwater incursion has once again increased. There are fears of a disastrous saline penetration of America's precarious Holland if the proposed Peripheral Canal is built and diverts more water.

The climate of the Delta is classified as being the cool and dry Mediterranean type, although to San Franciscans, the Delta in summer is hardly "cool." Westerly winds, almost as regular as Hawaii's trade winds, are sucked inland by the heat of the Valley, providing a natural air conditioning. The breezes bring cooling marine air to reduce Delta temperatures below those prevailing both immediately south and north. This maritime air, when combined with the great water surfaces, tends to temper the climate at all seasons. Extremes of heat and cold are rare. Lows from 13 to 17 degrees Fahrenheit have been recorded, and highs of 110 and even 114 degrees. But the January average is 40 degrees and July, only 75 degrees. For a brief period from the end of November to about December 10, there can be killing frosts, but all freezing is gone by February. (In late 1981, Delta folk were wishing that a frost might come, to kill off the massing floats of water hyacinth that are strangling marinas and narrow sloughs.)

Much more annoying today than either heat or cold in the Delta are the region's notorious tule fogs. Delta folk trapped in them find the dense, clammy, radiation fogs not only uncomfortable and depressing to one's spirits, but dangerous. The ground-hugging fogs blind motorists and cause many accidents and deaths. Sometimes, in a cold winter, a vast blanket of tule fog oozes out of the Delta, reversing the path of the summer's pleasant sea fogs, and spills over the Berkeley Hills into San Francisco Bay. The S.S. *City of Rio de Janeiro* blundered to her death on Fort Point Reef in the Golden Gate on February 22, 1901, in just such a "pea soup" of a tule fog.

Rain increases as you move north and northwest through the Delta from the ten inches received annually in the lee of Mount Diablo. About 80 percent of the rain falls between November and March. Precipitation is not so critical for winter field crops in the Delta as elsewhere, because of natural seepage and the availability of year-round irrigation. But it is important in leaching salts that accumulate in the soil.

The Delta's original cover consisted of hydrophytes and water-tolerant vegetation, with herbaceous annuals and perennial shrubs on higher and drier ground. The tops of the river and slough banks bore coarse bunchgrasses and willows, tangles of blackberries, wild roses, and wild grapevines. There were only shrubs above the tules of Sherman and lower Roberts islands, but the higher banks of Brannan, upper Union, and upper Roberts islands resembled parklands. Rows of oaks, cottonwoods, walnuts, and alders were joined by sycamores, particularly on the Mokelumne, and buckeyes on the Cosumnes. From Grand Island upstream, the Sacramento was so overhung with huge tree branches that they interfered with navigation by snagging the sails, yards, and rigging of passing vessels.

The dominant vegetation, the freshwater and often partially submerged tule bulrush, enjoys weathered peat and mineral-organic soils alike. Commonly, its annual growth of erect, unjointed, hollow stalks from a perennial root comes to a point six or eight feet in the air. The original *tulares*, or canebrakelike reedbeds, were highest and thickest in the Sacramento drainage. Vast jungles of the luxuriant reeds, gray greenish in summer, brown in winter, stood everywhere, broken only by curving channels and occasional circular ponds. Since reclamation, the tules are restricted to channels, sloughs, and overflowed tracts. Elsewhere, the bulrushes have been ousted by other plants. On the outer edge of artificial levees are willows, weeds, and thickets of blackberry vines (if the dikes manage to escape the scraping and rip-rapping of the Corps of Engineers); on the inner slopes are annual weeds and grasses.

The bottomlands of the streams that enter the Delta have vegetation similar to that of the high levees, including both the deciduous oaks and the liveoaks, or evergreen oaks, that once forested the Sacramento's natural levees. But southeast of the Calaveras River, a genuine prairie extends to the Stanislaus River.

In the old days, the Delta abounded with tule elk, antelope, and coyotes. Grizzly bears were frequent visitors, fishing during the annual salmon runs. (There is a Grizzly Island near Suisun City.) Here the mule deer of the Sierra and the black-tailed deer of the Coast Range met. Big game was mostly gone by the 1860s, hunted out by settlers and market hunters. But there were remnant bands of antelope on the nearby plains into the 1870s, and a few wary elk hid in the tulares till 1874. Small animals included the mink, land otter, and golden beaver that were trapped by American and French-Canadian mountain men (hence French Camp and Beaver Slough) in the 1830s and 1840s. The ubiquitous muskrat of today, also trapped, is not a native but a later introduction. Because of its levee burrowing, it is a pest in the Delta. But the excavating beavers are even worse in their weakening embankments. Some people blame both the 1972 Isleton and 1980 Jones Tract floods on beaver tunneling of peat levees.

The old Delta also teemed with badgers, raccoons, skunks, ground squirrels, gophers, cottontail rabbits and hares, or jackrabbits, woodrats and packrats, shrews, harvest mice and meadow mice, kit foxes, and wildcats.

Delta skies were darkened all day with flocks of ducks, geese, cranes (including the now-vanished sandhill variety), egrets, herons and blue herons, cormorants, whistling swans, flickers, woodpeckers, and western red-tailed hawks. Fleets of coots, or mudhens, "grounded" like kiwis, still bob about in their silly fashion in the sloughs. Once, brown and white pelicans were numerous and an Aleutian hunter with Kotzebue's exploring expedition in the 1820s was attacked by the big-billed birds after he shot one of their number. In 1841 Charles Wilkes, the U.S. Navy explorer, found waterfowl so tame in the Delta—Indians were able to club them with sticks—that he mistook some wild ducks and geese for barnyard fowl.

Honeybees long ago adopted the Delta for a home. John Muir, in a chapter entitled, "The Bee Pastures," of his classic book, *The Mountains of California*, wrote, "Out in the broad, swampy Delta of the Sacramento and San Joaquin Rivers, the little wanderers have been known to build their combs in a bunch of rushes, or stiff, wiry grass, only slightly protected from the weather, and in danger every spring of being carried away by floods."

Early visitors were less impressed with herds of tule elk, even sun-obscuring flocks of wildfowl, than with the Delta's clouds of vicious mosquitoes. In 1833, the Hudson's Bay Company fur trader, John Work, wrote of French Camp, "As we are here nearly surrounded by water, we are like to be devoured by mosquitoes." Capt. John Yates, recalling a Sacramento River visit of 1842, wrote, "I spent another night at the place and was engaged for nearly the whole of it in a desperate encounter with the mosquitoes." In January of 1850 it was Edward Wilson's turn to swat and curse, on the shore of Suisun Bay, "Mosquitoes abound here, of the largest and most venomous kind I ever felt."

A very welcome by-product of land reclamation was the abatement of the mosquito nuisance in the Delta.

Facing: Georgiana Slough

Low tide, Sacramento River

Reeds, Grand Island

Stump, Steamboat Slough

San Joaquin River

Winter storm, Andrus Island

Abandoned railroad bridge, Georgiana Slough

Delta grass, Snodgrass Slough

22

Miner Slough
Overleaf: Mount Diablo

TO EARLY EXPLORERS, THE VAST DELTA appeared to be sparsely populated by Indians. This was because they congregated in relatively few *rancherías*, the largest aboriginal villages in the state. They chose high and dry riverbanks or natural mounds, sometimes artifically enhancing them with berms. Even after decades of weathering, archeologists in the 1920s found mounds still raised to five feet above the normal level of the land. The Indians not only placed themselves above the rivers' flood stages, they also enjoyed good drainage in ordinary rainy weather.

Just as the Delta marked the confluence of two great river systems, so it was also the meeting place of two major Indian language groups—the Yokuts of the San Joaquin Valley, and the Wintun (Patwin) of the western Sacramento Valley and the Maidu of the eastern Valley. Sandwiched in between were Miwoks normally more at home in the plains, and especially the foothills, to the east.

West of the Delta were the Carquines who gave the strait its name; the Suisunes of the Benicia area whose headman, Sem Yeto, became the prominent Chief Solano of Mexican times; and the Chucumnes of the Rio Vista region. These and other nonresident tribes visited the Delta each year to fish during the annual salmon runs and to gather freshwater mussels.

The Delta held anywhere from three to fifteen thousand Indians, including those on the rimlands between the wet tulares, or tule fields and the bone-dry, treeless plains. The rimlands were often attractive parklands, grassy swards without undergrowth, dotted with

Part Two

Indians and Explorers

groves of liveoaks and white oaks, some of them three to four feet in diameter at the base. Not surprisingly, early explorers (like Fremont) and settlers alike preferred these areas to the swampy heartland of the Delta.

The largest rancherias, on the lower Sacramento River in the Sherman and Staten islands areas, held up to a thousand people. They were of rather short stature, but broad shouldered and strong. Dr. John Marsh in an 1846 letter said that the Delta Indians were heavier bodied and stouter than their kin east of the Sierra. Although the 1879 *History of Contra Costa County* described them as beardless, Marsh wrote, "They are a hairy race; some of them have beards that would do honor to a Turk." In any case, they were swarthy of complexion, with short, broad noses; low foreheads; and long, coarse black hair. Some, but not all, had the distinctive "almond eyes," or epicanthic folds, of Asians.

The Indians lived in conical huts of tule thatch. They also bundled the rushes to make *balsas*, reed canoes and rafts, and they used the stems for fiber—mats and cordages—while eating the roots, pollen, and seeds. But acorns, gathered in the fall, remained the staff of life. In winter, hunters took wildfowl. In the spring, if they had not fled to escape runoff floods, the Indians "grazed" on grasses, clover, and wild peavines, gleaned seeds, and dug roots and bulbs. The *torós*, "soaproot," was pounded for both food and soap. They also dug up the tiny bulbs of the brodiaea and *chuchupates* and *cocomites*, the roots and bulbs of wild iris. Early whites, aghast at seeing them eat grasshoppers, earthworms, and roots, derisively lumped all California Indians as Diggers, or Digger Indians.

Sacramento County historian Winfield J. Davis quoted an "expert" on Indians, Dr. M. F. Clayton, who was very much a product of his bigoted times. The good doctor, who called the Diggers "Tar Heads" because they made mourning marks of charcoal and pitch on their faces when they cremated their dead, wrote: "Their habits were those of laziness and filth, and they hardly had energy to steal. . . . They wandered about like tramps." In one respect, Clayton was correct—"The few attempts that have been made to civilize them have generally resulted in shortening their lives." So much for "civilization."

The so-called Diggers were many peoples. At least fifty genuine tribes, with distinct names, territories, and dialects existed among the Yokuts of the San Joaquin alone. They and the other Indians were broken into so many subtribes and bands that the early Spaniards identified them by the name of a major village, like Karkin on Carquinez Strait, or by the river whose valley they settled, hence the Cosumnes, Mokelumnes, and Tuolumnes. Many of the names carried over into the American period.

So different were the tongues of the Miwok and the Maidu, although both belonged to the Penutian speech family, that the explorer, Gabriel Moraga, turned back (1806) on the lower Mokelumne River because his interpreter could no longer make himself understood.

The Pulpunes, or Julpunes, occupied Dr. John Marsh's ranch near Brentwood, on the Delta's southwestern edge. The Ompines and Tarquimines occupied the often-overflowed low isles of the western Delta, the Quenensias, the large islands farther upstream. Two of the most important "metropoli" of aboriginal California were on the San Joaquin River. Passasimas lay either on Stockton Channel or Walker Slough. It was the antecedent of Weber's Landing, or Tuleburg, which became Stockton. On the San Joaquin's West Branch, better known as Old River, was Pescadero, The Fishery. This village of Yokuts people, called the Cholbones, was on Union Island east of modern Bethany. Other important Delta people were Juchiyunes, Coyboses, and Comistas.

The Yokuts and others hunted wild game with bows and arrows, using seven different bows for various prey. The best bows were of sinew-backed juniper, the staves traded from the Coast Range. Less perfect were bows of elderberry and laurel, or bay, wood. Two-piece arrows were tipped with points of obsidian, volcanic glass, traded from Sonoma and Lake counties. Hunters stalked deer while camouflaged or disguised by wearing deerskins and even antlered deer heads. Huntsmen also took elk and rabbits. They set fire to the tulares to drive out game. William Grimshaw, pioneer of the 1840s, recalled, "At night, the tules west of the Sacramento would sometimes be burning, and the elk and deer, running affrighted before the fire, would make a rumbling sound like distant thunder."

The Indians used nets, as well as snares, to take land animals, and all were skilled fishermen with nets, spears, and with hook, line, and sinker. The 1849 traveler Bayard Taylor understood why Pescadero was such an important place: "The salmon trout exceeded in fatness any freshwater fish I ever saw. They were between two and three feet in length, with a layer of pure fat, a quarter of an inch in thickness, over the ribs. When made into chowder or stewed in claret, they would have thrown into ecstasies the most inveterate Parisian gourmand."

The Yokuts, unlike some of their neighbors, ate dogs. But they had a taboo on eagles and other raptors, or birds of prey, and would not touch either coyote or grizzly bear meat.

The Indians knew how to use ash water to leach, in sand, the toxins from buckeyes and the tannin from acorn meal. There were no bedrock mortars in the marshy Delta, so they ground their meal in portable *manos* and *metates*, "mortars" and "pestles," for a mush called *chemuck*. The pestles were made of (scarce) stone, the mortars usually of wood. Seeds and acorns were stored in small granaries.

The Yokuts made excellent coil baskets of swamp grass and bunchgrass, stitching the layers together with bone awls. They fired no pottery vessels, but baked clay balls, or "doughnuts," that anthropologists believe were used in lieu of the cooking stones of other tribes — the "hot rocks" dropped into pitch-sealed baskets to make water boil.

The Delta's Indians had shamans, or medicine men, who were herb doctors as well as priests, magicians, and psychiatrists, and they made great use of the *temescal*, or sweat house, as a quasi-religious hospital, sauna, and lodge hall.

Cremation in funeral pyres was generally, though not universally, practiced by the Miwoks. Wintun burials, in either the outstretched or flexed positions, were often in sweat houses or village shell mounds. All corpses were placed with their heads to the west. After a death in the family, the Yokuts not only smeared their faces with a mix of pitch and ashes, but also burned their hair short in mourning.

The Indians liked to gamble with a guessing game, sometimes called "Hand," that was similar to the whites' shell game, usually two flat bones (sometimes sticks or shells), one plain and one marked with grooves. The women had a special game of their own, using black walnuts for dice. Athletic youths preferred a basketball-like contest. In this sport, a pole was tossed through a hoop rolling on the ground.

Governor Pedro Fages, in 1775, noted that each village chief, serving under a district chieftain responsible for four or five rancherias, wore a cloak decorated with feathers as a symbol of his office, and also a snood-like coiffure of false hair folded back over his own hair.

Commoners went naked except for, perhaps, a deerskin breechclout, sometimes painted and sometimes plain. Or they might wear a small cloak or cape reaching to the waist. In its folds, in place of pockets, they carried trifles, particularly small antelope horns holding tobacco. Smoking was very common. They wore braided cords or bands through their hair and imported shell beads or abalone shell pendants around their necks. Ear plugs were popular, too.

If they became cold, the Indians coated their bodies with thick layers of mud. In winter, they sometimes wore deerskin blankets, but no moccasins or other footgear. (Until the whites imported burrs and foxtails, by accident, there was only grass and tules underfoot.) Women wore a modest two-piece skirt, front and back of tules, willow bark, or buckskin. They tattooed themselves on the chin and face with charcoal dots and lines, and also pierced their noses for bone ornaments. According to Hermenegildo Sal, who soldiered in the tulares in 1775, *los gentiles*—"the savages"—were both robust and brave.

The Delta's Indians met Europeans in 1772, barely three years after the discovery of San Francisco Bay. Governor Fages gingerly explored the western periphery of the reedy wilderness with a chaplain-diarist, Father Juan Crespí. They took a muleteer, an Indian servant, and an *escolta* ("escort") of six Catalán Volunteers and six *soldados de cuero*, or leatherjacket regulars. The *cueros*, or jerkins, were really armor—the many layers of hide turned away Indian arrows. Frederick Beechey, the English explorer, wrote that the cowhide shields carried by the California soldiers would vie with that of Ajax in the number of folds of leather.

Spain's empire was stretched thin, and the number of *gente de razón* ("people of reason"—Spaniards) on Delta expeditions exceeded thirty-five only once, when fifty-eight Europeans marched into the tulares. Of course, fifty or a hundred Indian auxiliaries might accompany a party.

Fages found the water of Carquinez Strait to be fresh; he treated amicably with the Carquines Indians;

and he saw wildcats, panthers, or mountain lions, bears, wolves, and "buffalo." The latter must have been elk, though bison and wapiti are hardly look-alikes.

From a spur of Mount Diablo, probably Willow Pass, Fages was the first European to see the Delta proper. Father Crespí described it as a maze of islands, flat as the palm of one's hand, with channels cutting through great tulares. He thought that the San Joaquin River was composed of three *brazos*, or arms, that joined with the Sacramento at two level islands to create what he called the greatest river in New Spain. Soldiers familiar with the Ebro River in Spain swore that it was not half the size of the Sacramento at its mouth. Fages and Crespí named the lower Sacramento the Río de San Francisco, but the name did not stick.

That summer, 1772, Fages sent a corporal's guard into the Delta in pursuit of Army deserters from Monterey. The pursuers were ambushed by the runaway soldiers, who stole their horses and mules and fled up the San Joaquin. The governor sent out two more parties, and one squad overtook the deserters some fourteen leagues, or thirty-eight miles, upstream. Here the Delta claimed its first white victim. One deserter, to get away by swimming, jumped into a mire. He was swallowed up and, as Father Pedro Font learned in 1776, "He remained there, drowned and buried in the mud."

In September of 1775, Capt. Juan Manuel de Ayala had his first and second pilots, Don José Cañizares and Juan Bautista Aguirre, map the great *estero* ("estuary") as the Delta was then called. In the launch of the *San Carlos*, they sounded Suisun Bay and entered the San Joaquin, calling it the San Juan Bautista River. It appeared to be larger than the Sacramento, but it shoaled so quickly that the launch grounded, and they saw that it was clogged with sandbars and was unnavigable.

Cañizares was astounded by the skill of the Indian boatmen. The cigar-shaped tule balsas were so tightly woven that four fishermen in one, using double-bladed paddles, easily passed the chartmaker's *lancha* in spite of all the efforts of his straining, muscular oarsmen.

Next year, 1776, saw the land expedition of Capt. Juan Bautista de Anza, founder of California, with Lt. José Joaquín Moraga and Padre Pedro Font. They investigated twenty miles beyond Fages's penetration and found three rancherias. They also found deer and elk so abundant that the land, lined with well-beaten game trails, appeared to be occupied by herds of cattle, not wild beasts.

Like Fages, Anza was impressed with the Delta's fine balsas with their pointed prows and poops, and railings equipped with arched poles, "like a balustrade." As for Font, he admired the Indians' homes, large and well-made tule lodges.

From Oak Ridge east of Antioch, Anza led his men to the site of the Antioch Bridge and Oakley and Knightsen. His progress was blocked by the tule swamp of Rock Slough. He paralleled Old River to what later became Bethany, dodging pockets of miry tules, but then returned to Monterey via Patterson Pass.

In September of 1776, Moraga, Commandant of the San Francisco Presidio, invaded *Los Tules* by land.

He reached the San Joaquin River two or three days' march southeast of Antioch, expecting to rendezvous with a boat expedition. But his shortcut across the Diablo Range threw him far beyond the agreed-upon site. Francisco Quirós, Cañizares, and Padre Pedro Cambón, low on supplies, contented themselves with charting the lowermost San Joaquin River with the *San Carlos*'s launch, to False River.

Moraga made a fast march of three days up the San Joaquin, giving presents of beads to Indians, who welcomed him with gifts of fish and seeds and "great demonstrations of pleasure and friendship," and visited the Calaveras near its mouth at Stockton.

In November and December of 1776, Moraga accompanied Capt. Fernando de Rivera y Moncada to Old River, then called *Río del Pescadero*, or Fishery River. They pressed on to Middle River, termed the San Francisco Xavier, and then to the San Joaquin itself, called the San Miguel at the time.

In 1793 there was another boat reconnaissance, when Lt. Francisco Eliza explored with the *Activa*'s launch; and according to Diego Olivera, his father served on a forgotten Sacramento River exploration of 1798 or 1799.

Already, the Delta was becoming a refuge for *cimarrones*, or runaway mission (Christian) Indians, and their wild brethren. The latter were coming to be known as the Horsethief Indians because of their rustling of mission herds. The *gentiles*, or wild Indians, treated horses, mules, and cattle just as they did tule elk or mule deer; they were there for the eating.

The governor tried sending parties of Christian Indians to tame the Delta's savages by propagandizing, proselytizing, and converting. But these sorties were not very successful. For one thing, the aggressive neophytes sometimes kidnapped women and children in hopes of forcing the villages' men to come to so-called civilization. In 1795 the mission Indians were defeated in a battle, and they afterwards so alienated the Delta's inhabitants by their superior airs that the governor's practice became counterproductive. The handful of presidial soldiers had to be counted on to keep the peace; they soon demonstrated that faith in them was not misplaced.

When Father Pedro de la Cueva and the Indian *mayordomo* Higuera took three soldiers and some neophytes in 1805 to visit sick converts, hostiles killed four of the party, including one soldier, wounded everyone, and killed all of the horses, in a surprise attack in the Livermore Valley. Sgt. Luís Peralta administered swift, sure punishment on the guilty Pitemis Indians at a San Joaquin rancheria. He killed eleven men and captured thirty prisoners, mostly women. Chieftains of other wild tribes came to the Spaniards to assure them that they had had nothing to do with the attack.

The year 1806 saw three *entradas* into the wet hinterland, two by Spanish California's greatest pathfinder, Gabriel Moraga. The newly commissioned *alférez*, or ensign, was the thirty-nine-year-old son of J. J. Moraga, dark-complexioned, tall, and well built. Little is known of his first expedition, probably to the Mokelumne from Mission Dolores. On his second trip,

September, 1806, from Mission San Jose with Padre Pedro Muñóz, he found a stream full of butterflies, so he named it Mariposa Creek. He also discovered the Merced, Tuolumne, Stanislaus, and Calaveras rivers and located large and friendly rancherias, especially on the Calaveras.

Between Moraga's two marches, his second cousin, Alférez Luís Arguello, Commandant of the San Francisco Presidio, led an exploration of which little is known because Arguello's journal was lost.

There was another battle between Catholic and pagan Indians on Carquinez Strait in 1807, but the next real campaign (1808) was again Gabriel Moraga's. Although one of his charges was the selection of a mission site, he did not take a priest along. Moraga was also to explore, visit rancherias, bring in converts, round up runaways, and punish Horsethief Indians.

Moraga's troopers were well mounted and took remounts. Each man had an *escopeta*, or musket, a cartridge pouch, and a lance. Each wore a *cuero* of five thicknesses of sheepskin, a low-crowned, short-brimmed hat against the Delta sun, and leather chaps for pushing through dense woods and riverside thickets.

From *Laguna del Bravo*, between Tracy and Bethany, Moraga moved to Old River, then up the San Joaquin to a ford, passed a series of sloughs called *Lagunas de Guadalupe* (today's Finnegan's Cut-off), and reached the handsome meadows of the Stanislaus River, then called the Guadalupe.

En route to the Mokelumne, the farthest point of his 1806 expedition, Moraga hardly noticed the Cala-veras because of its seasonally dry bed, but he found a dozen heavily populated rancherias on the *Río de San Francisco* (Cosumnes) before he left the Delta without finding a single suitable mission site.

After an 1809 expedition by a Spanish sergeant and a possible Russian expedition from Fort Ross, the untiring Moraga was back in May, 1810, to punish the Suisunes for killing some Christian Indians. He was the first European to cross Carquinez Strait. Since he ferried his horses over, he must have used a ship's launch as well as the tule balsas later remembered by Governor Juan B. Alvarado (he was then a young soldier with the force). In the surprise attack on the village of Sespesuya, the soldiers killed all of the Indians holed up in two huts, but a third one held out. It was set afire by Moraga's Bolbones allies. "The valiant Indians died enveloped in flames, rather than surrender," the ensign reported. Most of the 125 warriors were killed, and Moraga set free the 18 captives since many were dying of their wounds. Moraga and his 4 wounded men were honored with pay increases and he was promoted to brevet lieutenant.

Moraga returned in August with Father José Viader, and in October stormed the Union Island rancheria of the Cholbones or Pescadores.

Fathers Ramón Abella and Buenaventura Fortuni led a boat party in October, 1811. After camping on Brown's Island at an old Indian fishing station, they went up Old River. They found that it bore the least water of the San Joaquin's three channels. In fact, it was no bigger than the Salinas near Monterey. It wound through swamps where there was nothing to see but blue sky and gray green tules. Landing from the boats was impossible, so the men slept aboard them.

The Spaniards passed several deserted rancherias, the populations having migrated, en masse, to Mission San Jose. They saw beaver tracks below Pescadero, which they thought might make a possible mission site, though it obviously flooded in winter. (Moraga and Viader had had to leave their horses a half-league from the fishery because the ground was so swampy.) Fortuni baptized a few Indians before following the shallow, log-jammed Old River to the Middle San Joaquin, three times deeper, and then to the main branch. Above its three forks, the padres found the San Joaquin a hundred yards wide and five yards deep in midstream. Abella urged all travelers to use the main river, to take the West Fork only if in pursuit of salmon or beaver.

The priests proceeded downstream to the big fishing rancheria of Passasimas—about 900 in population. They found that several villages had been hastily vacated upon their approach to the San Joaquin's Seven Mile Slough, which they followed to Three Mile Slough and the Sacramento River at the head of Sherman Island.

Descending the Sacramento past banks overgrown with walnut trees hung with wild grapevines, they spied wary natives. All were fearful of the strangers because of a rumor sweeping the Delta by "tule telegraph" that the Spanish had killed off the Cholbones. Villages of a thousand people were totally deserted. Abella and Fortuni rounded Decker Island and celebrated mass on the Sacramento's north bank near its mouth. It looked like an ideal site for a mission. Finally, the padres explored Suisun Bay, Nurse Slough, Montezuma Slough or Creek, and Suisun Creek, as far as Ulatis Creek. They thought that the Suisun area might be a good mission site, too.

The next explorations were by the military, strictly punitive parties hoping to capture fugitives or to punish Indian rustlers. Sgt. Francisco Soto led an 1813 pursuit of some apostates in Mission San Jose's launch. In October, he made a surprise dawn attack on a Cosumnes (or Usumnes) rancheria on the north end of Andrus Island. Four villages banded together to mass a thousand warriors against his dozen soldiers and one hundred Indian allies. The Indians fought tenaciously for three hours before fleeing into the tulares. Soto lost only one man, Julio, the Indian alcalde of San Jose. He praised his auxiliaries, "They threw themselves into the most dangerous portion of the battle, without any flagging."

In December, 1815, or January, 1816, Soto led another raid, but only as far as the Collinsville-Rio Vista area. No details are known except that some of his men mutinied when ordered into frail reed canoes.

Luís Arguello was the reluctant escort commander for an exploration by Fathers Abella and Narciso Durán in May, 1817, reluctant because he and Durán were not on speaking terms. Arguello's launch took the lead, but ran aground off today's Port Chicago and snapped its mizzenmast. The padres, meanwhile, spent an equally uncomfortable night on a half-submerged islet at the mouth of Montezuma Slough, trying to keep in the lee of the Montezuma Hills as a gale lashed the Delta.

After regrouping at Rio Vista, Arguello left the

tidal basin behind. He passed the villages of Cache Slough to ascend Steamboat Slough, which he mistook for the main channel of the Sacramento. Arguello named Grand Island, separating the slough and the Sacramento, *La Isla de los Quenensias,* for its Indians. He paid close attention to the west bank, where he saw the only rafts, as opposed to canoes, of the expedition. He battled the current up to the Freeport area, which Durán thought would be an excellent jumping-off point for the Sierra. Abella carved another of his crucifixes on a tree trunk to mark the spot. A battle nearly ensued there as a result of Spanish provocation. Because the villages emptied at their approach, troopers jumped ashore to try to catch watching Indians. Naturally, this was resented by the natives.

Around Freeport, Arguello reversed direction, probably because Durán insisted that they go no farther upstream. The Spaniards drifted down to about what is now Courtland, examining the left bank, and turned into flood-swollen Georgiana Slough, made passable despite its "rafts," or logjams, by high water. Several Indians were rounded up and baptized before Arguello gave them a speech and set them free. The expeditionaries then followed the North Fork of the Mokelumne to the San Joaquin.

Now Arguello split his company. He personally examined Brannan Island and Seven Mile Slough. While ostensibly searching for runaways, he seriously looked for timber for a new mast. Meantime, the priests headed for Passasimas after Sergeant Soto assured them that it was that *rara avis,* a village of friendlies who would not bolt at the approach of Europeans.

The priests traveled by night and rested during the heat of midday. They passed three large rancherias before reaching their destination, where they baptized a few converts and won promises from the Indians of a visit to the missions. The expedition was reunited when the clerics rejoined Arguello at the sand dunes, *Los Médanos,* east of Antioch.

Durán made no secret of his preference for the Sacramento over the San Joaquin River. He noted that the latter was wider, but carried much less water. He observed that even the marshy and lagoonlike parts of the Sacramento were full of Indian fishermen, while in all the San Joaquin "there is nothing but tule, without a tree under which the navigator may find shade, nor a stick of firewood with which to warm himself; whereas the Sacramento, when it is not flooded, has dry land on both banks, covered with poplar groves."

Sgt. José Antonio Sánchez left Mission San Jose in October, 1819 to recover stolen horses and ended up fighting a lively battle with Mokelumnes at the ford of the Calaveras River near today's Stockton. About twenty-seven hostiles were killed and twenty wounded, with sixteen taken prisoner. The noncommissioned officer recovered forty-nine horses. Sánchez had one of his Indians killed and five soldiers wounded, including the (later) well-known José María Amador. News of his victory spread through the Delta like a peat fire. The prisoners were set to work making adobe bricks at Mission San Jose, and Governor Felipe Solá not only praised Sanchéz but urged his promotion. Although already of retirement age, Sanchéz was honored by being made a brevet-alférez, or acting-ensign. He celebrated his promotion in 1820 by returning to recapture seventy stolen horses from the Cosumnes Indians.

Armed parties continued to invade the Delta after California became part of a Mexico independent of Spain, in 1822. Ensign Sánchez returned with Father José Altimira in 1823; and Otto Von Kotzebue, a German explorer in Russian service, went up the Sacramento in 1824. He admired particularly the savannas behind the thick screens of trees on the natural levees, "Steep banks sometimes opened to delightful plains where the deer were grazing under the shadow of luxuriant oaks." He also thought that the low ground was admirably adapted to rice cultivation.

Both the flora and the fauna intrigued Kotzebue. "All along the banks of the river grapes grow wild, in as much profusion as the rankest weeds; the clusters were large and the grapes, though small, very sweet and agreeably flavored." An Aleut with the German made the mistake of killing a pelican with his javelin, and an amazed Kotzebue reported, "The rest of the flock took this so ill that they attacked the murderer and beat him severely with their wings before other *baidars* came to his assistance."

Forays into the tulares by Christianized Indians resumed, but these expeditions often deteriorated into slave-stealing raids by corrupted neophytes. A much more intelligent policy was the missions' granting of leaves to their flocks, letting the Indians go home on vacation to mix with their kin in the interior. After secularization of the missions in 1834, many Christian Indians drifted back to the Delta and the region began to lose some of its primitive aspect.

The doughty Luís Arguello, second only to Gabriel Moraga as an explorer, took out the last major Spanish land expedition in October 1821. He mustered the strongest force yet to invade the Delta—two lieutenants, Chaplain Blas Ordáz, six artillerymen and a cannon, eighteen infantrymen, thirty-seven cavalrymen, native guides and interpreters, and even an English translator, John Gilroy. The latter was added, it was said, in case the party should march all the way to the Columbia River. Arguello's courage was unquestioned, but his geography was a bit shaky. More likely, he expected to run into maverick Hudson's Bay Company *engagés*, trappers who had drifted down into the Sacramento Valley from Oregon.

After launches ferried his men and a remuda of 235 horses across Carquinez Strait, Arguello pushed past Suisun Bay to a large rancheria on Cache Creek and another, Goroy, surrounded by grapevines, on the Sacramento's bank. There he picked up guides when he heard that the next villages upstream had been visited by mysterious *extranjeros*, or foreigners.

When he reached the three contiguous villages of Guilitoy, Arguello saw war signals—five puffs of smoke. He prepared for action as sixteen hundred Indians banded together in a unified force. After he fired some grapeshot and ordered a cavalry charge against them, they ran for cover. Five or six warriors were killed and others wounded. That night, arrows rained on the Spanish camp, where Arguello had doubled the guard. Miraculously, the only casualty was a frightened mule that slipped into the river and drowned because of its heavy packs. Arguello had eight divers try to salvage the lost ammunition and blankets, but they were unsuccessful.

After an October 27 truce and peace, the interpreter, Rafael, learned that the reported white strangers had not been on the Sacramento but on the coast. They were probably Russians from Fort Ross.

Arguello visited other important villages—Capay, Coru, and Chac, finding their citizens hospitable, before leaving the Delta for the northern Sacramento Valley and a march back to San Francisco via the Redwood Coast at Point Arena. So remarkable was his last great sweep through the interior that it was exaggerated into a so-called Expedition to the Columbia.

Ensign Sánchez, who was acquainted with every nook and cranny of the Delta after service in almost twenty Indian "escorts," or campaigns, was called upon in November, 1826, to repair the damage done by a bellicose Mission Indian alcalde. The latter tried to raid the Cosumnes Indians, but was defeated; he lost thirty-four men, almost lost his launch, and had his cannon captured. Sánchez burned the offending village and left forty-one dead Indians on the field. He lost only one man, a soldier whose *escopeta* burst in his face. "Citizen" Sánchez then penned a Napoleonic battle report—ludicrous in the eyes of Britisher Beechey—using gunpowder to make the ink!

The *California Star* was incorrect in designating Jorge as the first Indian horsethief, circa 1827. But the Laquisme, an ex–Santa Clara neophyte, was the most important rustler till Estanislao, or Stanislaus. Jorge was pursued after one of his raids and was killed. Stanislaus, who was ex-Alcalde of Mission San Jose, has recently been transformed, *à la* Murrieta, from renegade to patriot by revisionist historians. They see him as stubbornly resisting Mexican invasions of his *tierra* because of Mexican "plans" to seize, presumably via secularization, the horses and cattle held in trust for the Indians by the mission padres.

The last military reputation made in the Delta was that of Gen. Mariano Vallejo in 1829. He led a force against the apostate-warrior for whom the Laquisme River was renamed the Stanislaus. Supposedly, Stanislaus was planning to raid San Jose, and Vallejo moved to anticipate him. Horse stealing declined, temporarily, after Vallejo's pacification, although he was robbed of complete victory when the enemy slipped away in the night, and Sánchez's battle of the same year ended in a draw when the Cosumnes refused to be awed by his swivel cannon.

By 1833, the governor was again receiving complaints, and in 1836 Mission San Jose petitioned him for help against the Horsethief Indians. In 1839, Mission Santa Clara herds were raided, and Mission San Francisco de Solano's, at Sonoma, were next. But these were dying gasps of Indian hostility. Retaliation by Mexican soldiery would soon become unnecessary in the Delta. A new ally of the Mexicans appeared in 1833. It was a great epidemic of intermittent fever, malaria, possibly compounded by cholera, that was introduced by Hudson's Bay Company trappers. And, as a brutal coup de grace, the Delta's surviving Indians were swept by a smallpox epidemic in 1839.

The Indians died like flies. In 1879, local historians wrote that an Indian was rarely to be seen in Contra

Costa County, that there were probably only 50 left. San Joaquin County was worse. Census enumerators estimated that there were 379 Indians left in 1850, 41 in 1860, and only 5 in 1870.

The Mexicans not only had problems with Indians, but with Canadians and Americans "trespassing" in the Delta. The Canadian mountain men who came down the Siskiyou Trail from Fort Vancouver ranged all over the Delta in pursuit of beaver and land otter skins. But they were not the first on the scene. The American intruder, Jedediah Smith, was camping and trapping on the lower Stanislaus, which he called the Appellaminy, in the spring of 1827. The Mexicans renamed his Wild River the *Río de los Americanos* in honor of him and his *Yanqui* trappers, and it is the American River today. Confusingly, Jed Smith named the Calaveras the "Mackalumbre" and called the real Mokelumne the Rock River. To him the Cosumnes was Indian River.

When warlike Mokelumnes, emboldened after having repulsed a Mexican patrol, attacked some of Jed's men and broke up some traps to make iron arrowheads, he quickly "appeased" them, to use the words of Lt. Ignacio Martínez. It took just five shots by his *rifleros* ("riflemen," or sharpshooters), and five warriors lay dead in the tules.

Smith, trapped in the Pescadero area, floated his property across swollen watercourses on crazy balsa rafts of poles and reeds, then hunted Lone Tree Creek, soon to be called French Camp Creek. The area was such a morass that he had to build corduroy roads to extricate his packhorses, and his trappers had to take to canoes that they built of the skins of tule elk. He crossed the soggy, boggy Calaveras on a felled tree and cursed equally the mud and the grizzlies of the Delta. Twice his hunters shot bears but could not bring down the great beasts. After two men deserted, Smith decided to quit the swamp that the Delta had become after an incessant downpour; he headed north for higher ground.

Dr. John McLoughlin, the chief factor at Fort Vancouver, began to send annual trapping companies to the Delta in 1829. They were called the Buenaventura Brigades from a confusion of that mythical river with the Sacramento. Alex McLeod was the first "booshway" *(bourgeois)*, or brigade leader, in the Delta. He was not impressed. He called the Mokelumne the Quicksand River and soon went back up the Sacramento, leaving behind him only the place-name McLeod's Lake at Stockton.

In 1830, the more skillful Peter Skene Ogden detoured his Snake River Expedition to the San Joaquin, en route home to Fort Vancouver. He took a thousand pelts on the San Joaquin, which he mistook for the legendary "Boreantura," noting that "I trapped [it] from its source to its anchorage in the Gulf of San Francisco." To his surprise, Ogden ran into American interlopers in the Delta. Ewing Young had brought a party of trappers all the way from Santa Fe. For a spell, the Canadians and Americans hunted together.

Young, "fishing" (as the Mexicans put it) for beaver in the San Joaquin, was asked for help by a Christian Indian alcalde mounting an expedition against Chief Stanislaus's people, who had turned back Sgt. Francisco

Soto after fatally wounding him. Young's men whipped the Indians in a three-hour fight. Then Kit Carson and others raided the rancheria, routing the so-called Horse-thieves and burning their huts to the ground. The Indians countered by running off most of Young's animals. But they did not dream that Carson and others would make a hundred-mile pursuit to the Sierra. Kit and his comrades surprised them as they feasted, in presumed safety, on horseflesh. The trappers killed them all. Suddenly, the once-suspect Young was very much persona grata in Mexican eyes. But he took his company back to New Mexico in the fall of 1830.

Young's partner, William Wolfskill, returned in 1831 to settle on a Putah Creek ranch not far from the Delta. Young himself was back in 1832, building a canoe for a three-man beaver hunt. He found the Central Valley practically crowded. The Hudson's Bay men alone, Work and Laframboise, had 163 people.

When he captured two Indian horse thieves, Young dealt severely with them. He shackled them together in irons and beaver trap chains. They foolishly tried to escape by swimming a slough, where the weight of the metal dragged them down to death by drowning.

Young's men contracted malaria, but all recovered. They were shocked by the fever's depopulation of the Valley. J. J. Warner wrote: "From the head of the Sacramento to the great bend and slough [i.e., the Delta] of the San Joaquin, we did not see more than six or eight live Indians, while large numbers of their skulls and dead bodies were to be seen under almost every shade tree near water, where the uninhabited and deserted villages had been converted into graveyards." Even worse were the moans of the not-yet-dead. He could never forget "the cries of the dying, mingled with the wails of the bereaved, which made the night hideous in the 'Valley of Death.' "

By the summer of 1832, Michel Laframboise had established *El Campo de los Franceses,* later Castoria and French Camp. It served the Hudson's Bay Company as a seasonal bivouac site for many years. His hunt was a disappointing five hundred skins, so the French-Canadian moved to the high ground of Sutter Buttes early in 1833 to rendezvous with his *bourgeois,* an Irishman named John Work.

When the rains ceased in March, Work moved to Cache Creek, then to better trapping in the Cordelia area. He described the Delta as "a swamp overgrown with bulrushes and intersected in almost every direction with channels of various sizes." His men began to drop from malarial ague in the Suisun marshes and he lamented, "This disease again breaking out among us at this season is a serious evil, especially as we are without any proper medicines for it."

From the Suisun Creek and Woodland areas, Work —fighting malarial mosquitoes every inch of the way— forded the swollen Little Camas (Cosumnes) River to trap the Mokelumne from canoes. There were plenty of beaver, but they were "shy," hard to trap, and the tidal rise and fall made the staking of traps difficult. Still, Work kept his canoes out and the skins began to multiply. After he crossed the Calaveras on an Indian bridge, a toppled tree, he began to lose horses to Indian rustlers.

The men he hurried in pursuit lost the trail in the tules. Now he became suspicious of native guides. "Some Indians assisted me in seeking for the horses, but it is probable that they were seeking to lead astray, instead of aiding."

As if Work did not have enough trouble, two Indian wives ran away from their trapper husbands. But at least the Irishman found a horse heaven near French Camp, an elevated plain carpeted with clover. Also, though elk and antelope took to the water where they could not follow, his hunters managed to bag many animals.

When Indians stole more horses right under a guard's nose, Work commented in his journal: "We will be obliged to destroy a village or two of these scoundrels. So many of the men being absent in the canoes prevents me from going after and punishing them immediately. Besides, we are very scarce of ammunition."

The two runaway Indian wives, stripped naked by local redmen but otherwise unharmed, returned, but more horses vanished. When one of his Canadian-Indian trappers caught a horse thief in the act and shot him through the head, Work noted, sadly, "Notwithstanding our wish to pass through this country peaceably, we shall be obliged to go to war with these scoundrels."

When war came it was a skirmish on July 13, 1833. A Christian Indian with a gift of gab in Spanish, but also a forked tongue, led about twenty of his compatriots in a diversion, while others sought to steal more horses. When the thieves were seized by the alert Canucks, their comrades let fly with arrows. None of the trappers were hurt, and their rifle fire killed two of the hostiles while others, wounded, crawled off into the tules. But the small fight was a close call for Work. He wrote: "One of them had bent his bow to fire an arrow at me behind my back, but one of the women attacked him with an axe and he fled with the others."

Just before dawn, the Indians attacked again, loosing arrows into the Canadian camp from hiding places in the bulrushes. Work ordered his men to hold their fire in order to make their scanty powder and ball last. Just before first light, the ambushers gave a loud war cry, fired even more arrows, and melted away into the rushes. "Probably, they expected to find us asleep," mused the brigade leader, "and had not the courage to rush into the camp or wait till daylight, when they were sure they would not all escape." Miraculously, the only injury in camp was a horse wounded in the neck by an arrow.

As beaver returns dwindled and Indian hostility escalated into two more small battles, Work burned the forty huts of a chief recommended to him by the treacherous neophyte. Luckily, he had only one man wounded, and a second horse, in these affrays. He then pulled out of the Delta. His last comments were, "The visitation which this village has received may perhaps deter them from stealing again. On account of the scarcity of ammunition, we must defer punishing the other two villages for the present."

The march northward was a nightmare. Once-bustling rancherias were deserted, except for the dead and dying. He described the disease as a virulent tertian fever, another name for malaria. Although he gave all rancherias a wide berth, he lost some of his own men to the epidemic before he reached Oregon.

The sickness and the Indian hostility of the Delta discouraged Work. He practically wrote off the area as a future source of furs in his official report. "Our hunt only amounted to 1,023 beaver and otter skins. Indeed, the country is now so exhausted that little can be done with it." He later added, "My last expedition was the most unpleasant I have yet had. We had a good deal of trouble and some skirmishes with the hostile tribes of savages. . . . Worst of all, the fever broke out among my people."

The greatest of American beaver men, Capt. Joseph Reddeford Walker, was in the Central Valley in 1833 also, after having discovered Yosemite Valley. But he was forbidden by the Mexican authorities from trapping. On the promise of payment in recaptured horses, he joined a party in pursuit of mission runaways. But the veteran trapper was quickly disgusted by the brutality of his *Californio* hosts. They not only killed noncombatant women, children, and old men left behind in a rancheria, but cut off their ears as trophies, bloody souvenirs to prove their great "victory" to the people on the coast.

George Nidever and "Dutch George" Yount (actually Jundt), the founder of Napa Valley's Yountville, secured their discharges as Walker headed for home, convinced that the Valley was trapped-out. They took a boat crew of Sandwich Islanders on a two-month (1834)

hunt in the tulares of Suisun Bay and the Delta marshes. Yount later recalled only having had so-so luck, but Nidever always considered the hunt a "very fair success."

Camping on a dry strip of natural levee near some empty huts one night, Nidever heard a moaning from one of them. He looked inside. "I saw nothing at first but, my eyes soon becoming accustomed to the darkness, I made out a small child. . . . The little thing tried to talk to me. . . . She had probably been without food for three or four days. We took her to camp. I gave her a piece of boiled beaver and it was pitiful to see the eagerness with which she caught it to her mouth and sucked at it voraciously."

The two bachelors fed the child carefully, nursed her back to health, and made clothes for her. Yount tried to give her to a party of Indians. To his horror, they offered to kill the little girl for him when he declined their suggestion that he throw her into the river. (Perhaps they were of a different tribe and could no more understand the infant's few words than could the Americans.)

After carving their names on a tree trunk to mark the limit of their ascent of the San Joaquin, the trappers gave their Hawaiian boatmen orders to turn back for San Francisco Bay. Yount then took the girl home with him, after having her baptized and christened at Mission Dolores. The girl grew up and rejected several white suitors. She married an Indian and bore him several children before, alas, he murdered her.

Like Ewing Young, Yount and Nidever were deeply

depressed by the effects of the malaria that had, almost certainly, claimed the little girl's parents. The Dutchman believed that nowhere on earth was the fever more fatal than in the Delta. (Ironically, it was a blessing in disguise to the trappers. So devastated were the rancherias that game was everywhere and the unfished rivers teemed with salmon.)

Yount recalled the awful scene. "The poor, ignorant creatures knew no remedy. They resorted to their charms and flocked to the sweat houses and there, in groups of several hundreds, would dance frantically around a blazing fire and while thus dancing around, the malady would seize them and they would fall down in agonies of death till the sweat house could contain no more. . . . The bodies of untold thousands lay whitening the plains and fertile valleys. . . . So impregnated was the atmosphere with the effluvia of decomposing and putrifying bodies that it was almost impossible to navigate the rivers. Deserted and desolated villages stood tenantless all over the Valley."

The Delta was changed, though hardly tamed, by 1834. Depopulated of its *gentiles* by malaria, there was a compensating influx of ex-neophytes as the mission system crumbled. (Probably, many of them succumbed to fever, too.) But Capt. Edward Belcher in 1837 still described the naked gentiles as being "in the wildest state of nature."

When Ewing Young reappeared in 1834, it was not to trap but to begin a new era of California history by driving a herd of a hundred horses and mules up the east side of the Sacramento Valley to Oregon. Some of his herders were ruffians who seemed to delight not only in raping Indian women but in callously murdering their menfolk. The Delta was becoming "civilized."

In 1837, Young drove eight hundred longhorns up the west side of the Sacramento to the Willamette settlements. Young's clerk, Phillip Leget Edwards, exhausted by almost two weeks of effort in getting the rambunctious herd across Carquinez Strait, groaned a good-bye to the Delta. "*Adiós,* San Joaquin! Another month like the last, God avert! Who can describe it?"

Edwards, like his predecessors, was shocked by the effects of malaria on the Delta. Since his horse had to pick its way through skulls and bones, he observed, "On every hand we see revolting signs of its ravages."

That same busy year of 1837 the Royal Navy explored the Delta. Capt. Edward Belcher took H.M.S. *Sulphur*'s pinnace, two cutters, and a gig up the Sacramento. The Briton admired the tall timber on the river's banks and, like others, noted that "wild grapes in great abundance overhung the lower trees, clustering to the river, at times completely overpowering the trees on which they climbed, and producing beautiful varieties of fruit." (He picked some for dessert.) He had crewmen fell several oaks with axes, to measure them. One was twenty-seven feet in circumference, its branches not starting for sixty feet from the ground. He thought that the fallen giant was a noble sight.

Belcher's surgeon, Dr. Richard Brinsley Hinds, collected specimens of "tiger cats," wildcats, and coyotes (which he dubbed "jackal-foxes") while the commander himself studied the floodplains, "covered with the richest pasturage and interspersed with park-like groups of trees." Belcher sensed that there was a future for the Delta, though he felt that its trapping days were numbered.

Just three years after the Royal Navy, the French, in the person of Eugene Duflot de Mofras, explored the Delta and ascended the Sacramento to Sutter's Fort. In 1841, members of the U.S. Navy Exploring Expedition of Lt. Comdr. Charles Wilkes made a survey of the Siskiyou Trail from Fort Vancouver to San Francisco Bay. A boat party passed through the Delta while the land party of Lt. George Emmons and Midshipman Henry Eld skirted the marshes. They, too, were aghast at the destruction of the Delta Indians by malaria: "Their bones lay strewed about on the hills [i.e., Indian mounds] in all directions, there being not enough of the tribe spared—as we were told—to bury the dead. . . . In one of the skulls a bird had built its nest."

Belcher's obituary for the Delta fur trade was premature. Laframboise, nicknamed Captain of the California Trail, was spectacularly successful, perhaps because he had a girl (Indian) in every "port" of the Delta. In 1835–36 he hunted from a hideaway on a Delta island, hoping to escape the notice of the Commandant of the Northern Frontier, Gen. Mariano Vallejo. Both Vallejo and Governor José Figueroa tried to restrict his hunts, but he paid them little attention. Laframboise's spring hunt in 1837 was worth an astounding £2,314. In 1838 he took out 1,361 large and 225 small beaver, plus 884 otter. The next year was even better, with 1,590 beaver pelts.

Capt. John Sutter bought fine moccasins, shirts, and pantaloons of deerskin from the Canadians' Indian or half-breed wives—and, secretly, traded *aguardiente*, brandy, for Honourable Company "plews," or pelts. At the same time, he protested British incursions into Mexican territory—whose beaver, of course, he hoped to monopolize. Sutter described a Laframboise encampment, probably at Trappers' Camp (French Camp), as resembling a large and permanent tent city.

A priest in Oregon, probably Father Blanchet, wrote of the "revolting exteriors" of Laframboise's followers, the brigade being "a hideous assembly of persons of both sexes, devoid of principles or morals." But other observers, like, surprisingly, Rev. Elijah White and the first woman historian of Oregon, Miss A. J. Allen, who paraphrased the preacher, found the Delta's trappers to be more romantic than scoundrelly in appearance: "The style in which they traveled was rather novel, bringing with them beds, bedding, tea, coffee, sugar, bread, cheese; not even the wine was left behind. . . . They formed themselves in Indian file, led by Mr. La Fromboy, the chief of the party. Next to him rode his wife, a native woman, astride—as is common with females—upon her pony, quite picturesquely clad. She wore a man's hat with long black feathers fastened in front and drooping behind her very gracefully. Her short dress was of rich broadcloth, leggins beautifully embroidered with gay beads and fringed with tiny bells, whose musical tinkling could be heard at several hundred yards distance. Next, the Clerk and his wife, much in the same manner, and so on to the officers of less importance and the men and, finally, the boys driving the packhorses with bales of furs, 180 pounds to each animal. The trampling of the fast-walking horses, the silvery tinkling of the small bells, the rich, handsome dress and fine appearance of the riders, whose numbers amounted to sixty or seventy . . . had quite an imposing appearance."

By 1840, with the hunt seriously declining, Laframboise was also tiring of the long marches to the Delta from Fort Vancouver on the Columbia River. He had to face the opposition of Vallejo, the governor, Sutter, and sometimes also, the enmity of the Indians. When the authorities finally, and grudgingly, licensed foreigners to trap if they became Mexican citizens with passports and proved themselves *"hombres de providad y buena conducta"* ("men of probity and good conduct"), Laframboise found his men becoming so ruffianly and mutinous that he actually feared for his life at their hands.

Francis Ermatinger replaced Laframboise. He found the Delta a vast bog in 1841, but hunted there and on Cache Creek and on Wolfskill's Suisun Valley ranch. He sent out parties with orders to rendezvous with him by April 25, 1842—"The latest date at which the swarms of mosquitoes would allow them to carry out their trapping in the haunts of the beaver and the otter."

Ermatinger's catch was so poor that Dr. McLoughlin decided to send Laframboise out on two final hunts, then call it quits in the Delta. Michel did not do well, either, and—symptomatic of changing times—when he said *adiós* to the Delta for the last time, in May of 1843, he simply sent his furs to the new Hudson's Bay Company trading post-store in San Francisco, rather than laboriously packing them to Fort Vancouver.

Capt. John Sutter finally had his fur monopoly in 1844, and he sent forty trappers into the Delta. But it was too late. Not only was the area pretty well trapped-out, but emigrants were coming down the Sacramento Valley portion of the Siskiyou Trail as well as over the Sierra from "the States." Some of his own lieutenants were taking off to set up ranches of their own to the north and east of the Delta.

In 1846, Sutter had a new problem. Renegade Mokelumnes, recovered from the malaria, ran off the horses in the corral of his chief trapper, Pierson B. Reading. Sutter, already siding with the Americans as the Mexican War loomed, guessed that Gen. José Castro had incited them. In June, he and Reading led a last punitive expedition into the Delta. One of their rafts capsized in crossing the Mokelumne River with considerable loss of arms and ammunition. Sutter attacked the Indians in a cave on the Calaveras River but had to withdraw when his diminished supply of powder and ball gave out. However, he put a price on the head of the renegade leader, Eusebio, and Chief Pollo ("Chicken") later brought in the raider's scalp.

The real coup de grace for the Delta's fur trade came in 1848–49 with the Gold Rush, hard on the heels of the disruptive Mexican War. It turned the California economy upside-down and flooded Alta California with a tidal wave of Argonauts. A few of them, disappointed in the gold mines, even drifted into the marshlands to squat in clearings on high ground, to become the first white settlers of the Delta.

Facing: Thomas Dean home, Sacramento River

Henry Myers home

44

A. T. J. Reynolds home

Wagon and barn

Rosebud Farm, home of William Johnston

Barn, the O. R. Runyon farm

Barn door, Twitchell Island

Night view, Locke

Community gardens, Locke

Walnut Grove

Bank of Alex Brown, Walnut Grove
Overleaf: Star Theater, Locke

BEFORE GOLD MINING, THE SACRAMENTO WAS a limpid stream. Edwin Bryant, who likened it to the Delaware, wrote in 1846, "A more beautiful and placid stream of water I never saw." But, aside from scattered Indian rancherias, the Delta was a no-man's-land in Spanish and Mexican times.

The closest settlements were neither missions nor civil pueblos but land grant ranchos. Governor Manuel Micheltorena in one year (1844) approved thirty-three petitions in the Sacramento Valley alone, to curry support for his crumbling regime. But no one wanted land in a swamp—which the Delta was, before reclamation. Eventually, ranches ringed the fenland, but few penetrated it, and their effect was minimal.

José Noriega, who had received Rancho *Los Méganos* ("Sand Dunes") in 1835, sold it in two years to Dr. John A. Marsh for five hundred dollars. Marsh renamed it *Los Pulpunes* for the Indians of the Brentwood-Antioch area. Soon, he had neighbors in José Megill and José Antonio Mesa of another Sand Hills Ranch, this one spelled *Los Médanos.*

In 1839, Capt. John Sutter founded *Nueva Helvetia*, "New Switzerland," or Sutter's Fort, distant from the Delta on the American River near its junction with the Sacramento. But Sutter's influence soon predominated in the Delta. The Mexican authorities favored New Helvetia as a bastion against the incursions of Indians, Russians, and Canadian and American fur trappers. Virtually all traffic through the Delta before the Gold Rush was bound to or from Sutter's colony.

Compared to John Sutter, Marsh was a "tough

Part Three
Squatters and Settlers

customer." He was feared and respected, but not loved, by the whites whom he bullied and the Indians whom he whipped. He ran horses and cattle, continued Noriega's garden, and added a vineyard. His main interests, like Sutter's, were not in the marshy Delta. But he told Edwin Bryant that he had explored the San Joaquin River from its source to its mouth. His adobe was less a place of refuge for distressed American emigrants arriving in California than was Sutter's Fort because the skinflint demanded cash for his succor, whereas the Swiss was a generous and compassionate man.

In 1844, Marsh became more than a rival of Sutter's; he became his enemy. The latter shanghaied him into a foreign legion mustered at Sutter's Fort for Governor Micheltorena's disastrous campaign against rebels. Marsh neither forgave nor forgot. But he had just twelve years to nurse this grievance because, in 1856, three vaqueros, exasperated at his abuse—and low wages—murdered him.

For all of the explorations of Moraga and Arguello, the Delta was largely terra incognita still, in 1839. On his first expedition into the Delta, John Sutter could not find an experienced river pilot in San Francisco. So he chose a young but skilled half-Hawaiian, Capt. William H. (Kanaka Bill) Davis. Sutter's party was composed of half a dozen whites, six or eight *kanaka* (Hawaiian) men and women, and a bulldog from Honolulu. "Billy" skippered a fleet consisting of the schooners *Isabel* and *Nicolás*, armed with two brass cannon as well as small arms.

Every evening, Sutter halted to explore inland for a colony site. It was not pleasant work. Davis recalled:

"When stopping along the bank of the river at night, we could not obtain any rest on account of the immense multitudes of mosquitoes which prevailed, exceeding anything we ever experienced before."

Sutter was met by seven or eight hundred Indians just below the site of Freeport, and the whites and Sandwich Islanders prepared for an attack. But the Indians were not hostile, merely curious. They made no attempt to stop Sutter from erecting a cluster of tents on the American River near the Sacramento as his Hawaiians began building *hale pili*, grass shacks, the antecedents of the great adobe bastion of Sutter's Fort.

The Sacramento River curved through a howling wilderness in 1839, as Davis reported: "As we moved away, Captain Sutter gave us a parting salute of nine guns—the first ever fired at that place—which produced a most remarkable effect. As the heavy report of the guns and the echoes died away, the camp of the little party was surrounded by hundreds of Indians, who were excited and astonished at the unusual sound. A large number of deer, elk, and other animals on the plains were startled, running to and fro, stopping to listen, their heads raised, full of curiosity and wonder, seemingly attracted and fascinated to the spot, while from the interior of the adjacent wood, the howls of wolves and coyotes filled the air, and immense flocks of waterfowl flew wildly about over the camp."

Sutter, at first, had only a four-oared boat to make the transit of the Delta to San Francisco Bay. But in 1841, he bought Fort Ross from the Russians and took over their schooner, renaming it the *Sacramento*. For several years it was the only vessel to ply Delta waters. William Grimshaw, skipper of the kanaka-crewed *Susanita*, a decked-over ship's longboat, remembered seeing the schooner so heavily laden with wheat in bulk that the grain slopped over the coaming of the hatches. By 1844, according to John C. Fremont, Sutter also had a large two-masted lighter. By 1848, a tiny flotilla would anchor at Sutter's Embarcadero, where Sacramento stands today—the *Sacramento*, William Leidesdorf's *Edwards*, and Captain Winner's decked boat.

The *Sacramento* was captained first by John Yates, a drunk; then by Lewis Keseberg, a cannibal (with the Donner Party); and next by Heinrich Lienhard, Sutter's ingrate aide, who always had an unkind word for someone. The *Sacramento*'s kanaka crewmen, for a long time, were the only knowledgeable navigators of the Delta. Lt. Edward F. Beale was so disgusted with one incompetent captain that he took his launch away from him and left him in the tules. Edwin Bryant, in 1846, was told that navigators got lost for days in the "terr-aqueous labyrinth" and that some perished in the tules and were never found. William Grimshaw recalled that, as late as 1849, "the shores of the San Joaquin from the Stanislaus to Marsh's Landing [now Antioch] at its mouth were a wilderness. Not a house did we pass [in] the whole distance, nor did we even see an Indian, to break the monotony of the trip. . . . Incompetent pilots . . . would enter some one of the networks of sloughs between the Sacramento and San Joaquin and row about for days before they were extricated from the labyrinth."

The Sacramento was more traveled by pre–Gold Rush Californians than the San Joaquin, and was a much more handsome stream. But navigation on it was hardly a pleasure, for all of the fine scenery. Grimshaw had to camp on the bank of Steamboat Slough one night in April, 1849, when the curiously named *Dice Mi Nana* ("Says My Momma") tied up. "No description can do justice to the misery of a night thus passed in the warm months. Clouds of mosquitoes rendered sleep utterly out of the question, no matter how hard a man had worked all day at the oar, or otherwise. The only way of getting through the night was to build a fire which could make as much smoke as possible, and walk about until morning, flopping a handkerchief before the face."

Bayard Taylor, also traveling in 1849 without a mosquito bar, tried another technique on the San Joaquin. He wrapped a blanket around his head to keep the blood-sucking insects away, and managed to fall into a fitful, half-smothered sleep. When he awoke, groggy, at midnight, he found an enormous full moon hanging over the Delta. He wrote: "Surely, the moon has been bitten by mosquitoes, and that is the reason why her face is so swollen and inflamed."

When men left Sutter's employ to establish their own ranches, they usually went north on the Sacramento or east on the Mokelumne or Cosumnes rivers, not into the Delta. As for the old Cholbones fishery southwest of French Camp, it was the focus of twin grants, Rancho del Pescadero and Rancho Paso del Pescadero. Valentín Higuera and Rafael Felíz owned the first one, 1843–46, but just let cattle run wild on it. It was not patented (to Hiram Grimes) till 1858. The grant at the "pass" (ford) of Old River was owned by Antonio M. Pico, but he never occupied it. Coclaimant Henry M. Naglee patented it in 1865.

When John Bidwell, Sutter's chief aide, made a map for the governor in 1844, he showed only two ranchos really *in* the Delta. One was his own Los Ulpinos, or Sillac, grant of 1844 near today's Rio Vista. The other was William Gulnac's Rancho Campo de los Franceses, from the Calaveras River to French Camp Creek. (On the San Joaquin near the Stanislaus, Bidwell showed a nonexistent Rancho de Livermore y Amador; he was a victim of hearsay.)

On his four leagues, Bidwell landed an English foreman and some ranch hands to winter over while building an adobe and cultivating a plot. Jacob D. Hoppe, an ex-Marylander who ran the pioneer newspaper the *Californian*, urged Bidwell to develop a real immigrant colony there in 1846, along the lines of New Helvetia. He suggested that it be named Brazoria, or Sacramento Brazoria, from *brazos*, the "arms" of a river. Bidwell invited some travel-worn immigrants to make it their home, but they stuck it out only till the spring of 1847. Then Bidwell wheedled a few Sutter's Fort settlers to shift to his nascent colony, but they nearly starved to death during a bad winter. Small wonder, the Indians called the area *Hale Chemuck*—"Nothing to Eat."

Although the grant's terms forbade sale or encumbrance, Bidwell just waited till California became American and sold off the rancho in small holdings.

Gulnac's ranch took its name from the camp of the French-Canadian trappers of the Hudson's Bay Company. He was a naturalized Mexican citizen but, since he could find no Mexican-Californians who would serve as tenants, he hired three Americans to fulfill residence requirements. They took charge of his horses, mules, tame cows, and a herd of a hundred half-wild beef cattle. The hands put up a corral at old French Camp and an adobe ranch house near the base of the Stockton Channel.

During the 1844 anti-Micheltorena revolution, two of the men left the ranch. The remaining *Americano* was murdered in February or March of 1845 by Indians who ran off the stock. Gulnac's business partner, Charles M. Weber, then bought the property at very much of a bargain price—48,747 acres for two hundred dollars.

Weber came to California in 1841 with the Bidwell-Bartleson Party of emigrants. After working for Sutter, like so many Delta pioneers, he struck out for himself as a San Jose merchant and cattleman. Leonard Kip, brother of the Episcopal bishop of California, considered Weber to be scarcely less distinguished than Sutter himself. It was Weber who urged Gulnac to petition for the grant. He had seen the land, the Frenchman had not. But Weber was not a Mexican citizen and could not file.

Continuing Indian scares prevented Weber from persuading anyone to occupy the place till 1847, though he enjoyed the friendship of a local chief, Cacoax. He then built corrals for two thousand head of cattle that he trail-herded up from San Jose. He next opened a store and surveyed the site of his town of Weber's Landing, later Tuleburg. It was finally renamed Stockton in honor of a Mexican War commodore.

By October, 1847, Tuleburg held twenty-five vaqueros, plus hired Indian ranch hands. Weber imitated Sutter in cultivating wheat and other crops as well as raising cattle. At 1848's end, his village of a hundred families was prospering in a modest revival of a trade of mission days. He hauled hides and tallow to San Francisco on a schooner new to the Delta, the *Maria.*

When the Gold Rush broke in 1848, Stockton shortly became the freighting center for the Mother Lode mines, its streets crowded with Mexican muleteers. When James Carson first saw the place, it was largely Joe Buzzel's tule-thatched log cabin. But when he returned on May Day 1849, there were so many tents that he called it "a vast linen city." Leonard Kip found a gallows but no courthouse, only a makeshift "city center" aboard an old brig moored to the landing. The poop deck served as a courtroom, the cabin was the jury room. The hold was the prison, and the forecastle, the town's hospital.

John W. Audubon, son of the great bird artist, found the mushroom town of tents and skeletal houses disappointing. It was situated on land as level as that of Houston or the levee country of Louisiana; each shower left deep mud. He thought that the canvas Exchange Hotel should be renamed The Exchange of Blacklegs because there were so many villainous fellows at the gaming tables. Stockton prices were beyond belief— flour at forty dollars a barrel, pork at sixty-five; pilot bread was twenty cents a pound and rubber boots, essential in the Delta, were going at fifty to sixty dollars the pair. Tents worth twelve dollars in "the States" cost forty dollars. Audubon was happy to move on. "None of us regrets leaving Stockton," he wrote. But even leaving was difficult. A southeast gale blew his boat ashore twenty times (he estimated) in the first hour after leaving the wharf, and finally deposited it, for two days, high up in the tules.

Most of the Central Valley's hundred and fifty Americans of 1846 were at Sutter's Fort, with a few at Marsh's Ranch and along the Mokelumne, Cosumnes, and Calaveras rivers, on small ranchos or at key fords on the trail to San Jose. A couple of *Yanquis* perched on Putah and Cache creeks, and a lone ferryman was at Montezuma, near the Sacramento's mouth.

Just one solitary soul lived in the heart of the Delta, the eremitical William Clements. At Sutter's Fort in 1845, by 1846 he was squatting in a hut on the Sacramento's left bank forty-three wriggling miles by water from the fort. His only companions were his Indian wife and several half-breed children.

A much more successful squatter lived on the north edge of the Delta near later Clarksburg. He was John L. Zwart, a Dutchman universally called Schwartz. He called his place, rather grandly, *Nueva Flandria,* "New Flanders," in bald imitation of Sutter's New Switzerland. But it was never confirmed as a land grant.

Zwart raised potatoes and a few other vegetables and can be considered the founding father of Delta truck gardening. But he also shared with Sutter the honor of establishing California's fishing industry, two decades before the first (1864) Sacramento River salmon cannery at Rio Vista. Gillnetting of Chinook, or king, salmon eventually became big business, until commercial fishing was outlawed on the river. Even before the Mexican War, Sutter was exporting salted salmon to the eastern states and Hawaii. His lieutenant, Pierson B. Reading, estimated that 10 percent of the salmon run was taken by the gill-netters. Zwart hired a gang of Indians to net the salmon with seines stretched across the river by canoes, then to pickle or dry the catch.

Zwart, like Weber, came to California with the Bidwell-Bartleson Party in 1841. Lienhard described the middle-aged bachelor as "a queer person." Edwin Bryant agreed. "Our host, Mr. Schwartz, is one of those eccentric phenomena rarely met with." The Dutchman had forgotten his own language without really acquiring another as a substitute. When Bryant asked why fifty barrels of pickled salmon in a shed were spoiled, Zwart tried to explain but quickly "lost" his visitor with his babble. Bryant described his talk as gibberish, "a tongue (language it cannot be called) peculiar to himself and scarcely intelligible. It was a mix of French, German, English, Spanish and rancheria Indian, each syllable of a word sometimes being derived from a different language."

Bryant found the Delta pioneer's place on October 25, 1846, to be a tule-thatched cottage about twelve feet by twenty. "We found a fire blazing in the center of the dwelling on the earth floor and suspended over us were as many salmon, taken from the Sacramento, as could be placed in position to imbibe the preservative qualities of the smoke. . . . Stretching ourselves on the benches surrounding the fire, so as to avoid the drippings from the pendant salmon, we slept till morning, when Mr. Schwartz provided us with a breakfast of fried salmon and some fresh milk. On the banks of the river, the Indians were eating their breakfast, which consisted of a large fresh salmon, roasted in the ashes or embers, and a kettle of *atole* made of acorn meal. The salmon was four or five feet in length and when taken from the fire and cut open presented a most tempting appearance. The Indians were all nearly naked and most of them having been wading in the water at daylight to set the seines, were shivering with the cold whilst greedily devouring their morning meal."

On Heinrich Lienhard's first passage in the schooner *Sacramento*, Capt. John Yates, drunk most of the time, halted at Zwart's for a salmon bake. With his usual sarcasm, Lienhard called the Hollander's humble cabin "a palatial villa, set in a secluded jungle retreat inhabited mainly by wolves and gray bears." But he enjoyed his free meal. "It was the first time I had ever tasted this fresh, pinkish meat; although it was cooked only in hot ashes, yet it provided a gala repast. I do not know who paid for the fish, but I had been invited to the feast and accepted with alacrity."

Returning upriver in February, 1847, Lienhard grew bored with the schooner's slow progress against a rapid current. Yates, superstitiously, tried to "whistle up a wind" but had no luck. Also tired of the company of the "fat, pompous little Englishman," Yates, whose drunkenness sometimes landed him in the *calabozo* and once (1844) piled the schooner on the rocks, Lienhard decided to abandon ship.

With a big-talking Kentucky rowdy, James McDowell, Lienhard decided to strike overland through the Delta to Sutter's Fort via Zwart's clearing. They would accompany an Indian runner taking a message to Sutter. Lienhard was sensible enough to know that the overland march would be arduous. He described the riverbank near their departure point, Bill Clements's shack, as a thick jungle of oaks, poplars, cottonwoods, ash, sycamores, and willows screening stretches of swamps thick with tules and other reeds that extended deep into the backcountry. It was, he wrote, "the haunt of wild animals, including grizzly bears, wolves and a species of wildcat."

Lienhard urged McDowell to take blankets, and matches for a campfire. But the braggart scoffed at the idea; he did not plan on any camping. "When I travel," he boasted, "I travel! I am not too lazy to keep moving, and do not intend to stop or camp before I hit Sutter's Fort." So Lienhard took no matches and only one blanket and a knapsack.

The Indian broke trail with McDowell hot on his heels and the young Swiss bringing up the rear. The hikers had gone only yards before their path was blocked by a knee-deep slough which they had to wade. They kept to the grassy areas of the natural levee between the forest on the river's edge and the tule swamps of the hinterland. But the long-legged, fast-walking, and loud-talking Kentuckian's pace soon slackened. He sug-

gested a rest. Since they had covered barely six miles out of forty, Lienhard refused to stop. McDowell then complained of pains in his legs. "I'm very lame," he whined. He fell behind as Lienhard trudged after the Indian, saying that he was not going to stop till he reached the Indian village across the river from New Flanders, about twenty-nine miles distant.

Lienhard found the Delta's tule marshes submerged with deep water and his way blocked by "lagoons," sloughs, of various depths and breadths. All were flowing swiftly into a Sacramento tugged along by ebbing tides. The three men laboriously waded several marshy sloughs where cold water reached to their hips and, a few times, to their shoulders. "These icy baths I did not enjoy," recalled Lienhard. A few of the backwaters were too deep to ford, but the travelers were able to cross them by using the overhanging branches of huge trees. McDowell kept finding superb places to camp, but Lienhard refused to listen to him.

At first, the travelers met only coyotes, wildcats, and deer. However, as Lienhard hopped down to the bank of a slough from an overhanging branch, he noticed a large number of "buzzards" (turkey vultures), magpies, and crows, or ravens, perched patiently—as if awaiting a meal—in the tree. As McDowell scrambled clumsily to the ground with a thud, he released a branch that whipped back noisily. Suddenly, all of the birds took off and the men heard a growling whistle from the brush.

The Indian froze. On tiptoes, he peered all around. A nervous Lienhard asked him, "Is it a wolf?" "No," he answered. "Is it an elk?" "No, no." Lienhard persisted, "Is it a grizzly bear?" "Yes," whispered the Indian.

Now Lienhard learned that McDowell, armed to the teeth with a rifle, two pistols, and a bowie knife, had not loaded any of his arms. The Swiss drew his own hunting knife, prepared to defend himself. He ordered the Indian forward. Naturally, the courier refused. But Lienhard gave him a rude shove and the two whites hurried after him. There was no attack, but Lienhard wrote in his memoirs, "Why the gray rascal allowed us to escape unmolested is a mystery."

Remembering the hospitality of the salmon bake, Lienhard did not want to rest in a vermin-infested Indian hut when they reached the rancheria. He borrowed a canoe of Zwart's and crossed to the west bank. Damp, chilled, exhausted, and ravenously hungry, he knocked on the door and asked for food and lodging. Zwart gave him salty smoked salmon and an unpalatable liquid that he called coffee, but which Lienhard likened to dishwater. Still, he ate heartily.

When he asked for the loan of some bedding, the Dutchman told him that he had no right to lend the hammock and blankets left in his care by a fellow Hollander. So the tired young man shuddered in his sodden clothing under his one thin blanket on a bed that was a five-foot bench about a foot wide. Sleep was impossible for the wretched traveler. "Through the various cracks and openings in the hut a sharp, cold southeast wind blew, and the fire of willow logs gave out comparatively little warmth." Slowly, excruciatingly, the night wore on.

At dawn, Zwart prepared a breakfast identical with the supper of the evening before, over-salted salmon and weak coffee. Lienhard explained that he had no money, but was so embarrassed at the look of resentment on his host's face that he offered him a cup that he treasured because of its associations. He told Zwart, "I gave my last piece of silver for this tin cup in Independence, Missouri, and I should like to keep it; but I am willing to give it to you if you think you should be recompensed for your hospitality."

Zwart gargled something in his strange jargon. Lienhard, without the foggiest idea of what his response was, asked, "What are you saying?" It was evident from the Dutchman's sign language, not his babbling, that he was covetous of the cup. So Lienhard, disgustedly, gave it to him.

Young Lienhard not only cursed the hermit for his lack of true hospitality, he later blamed him for the failure of Sutter's garden at Mimal. "The potatoes, which had large runners, had weak roots. The seed came from the Dutchman, Schwartz, and was so poor that there was little chance for a good crop."

Old Zwart was the Delta's first success story, by 1849. Bayard Taylor said of him, "We passed a ranch, the produce of which in vegetables alone was said to have returned the owner, a German by the name of Schwartz, $25,000 during the season." Peter H. Burnett, first governor of California, wrote that he found plenty of melons in Sacramento City, that summer of 1849, because "an old man of the name of Swartz cultivated several acres of them on the west bank." According to

Burnett, Zwart sold them readily for a dollar to three dollars apiece, depending on size, and made $30,000 from melons alone that year. "Such times," wrote Burnett, "I think, were never seen before and will hardly be again."

Edward Wilson, in his *Travels in California* (1852) was also impressed by the Delta hermit. "There are only some few huts and wooden houses scattered along the margin of the river, but by far the most remarkable, both for itself and its proprietor, is the ranch of Antonio Swartz, at present one of the wealthiest men in that part of the country. Mr. Swartz has a large patch of ground under cultivation and employs a detachment of a tribe of Indians to cultivate it. His farm lies eight miles on this side of Sacramento City and he enjoys a monopoly of market vegetables. He is Swiss (I believe) by birth, but is conversant with almost all languages."

In another version of his travels, *The Golden Land* (1852), Wilson added: "From some confusion in his memory, [Zwart] usually employs two or three different tongues in every sentence. No one can tell by what means he got ascendancy over these Rancheros, or half-civilized Indians; but it is certain that they work for him faithfully and with a wonderful (for an Indian) industry, whereas no one else can induce them to do anything but vagabondize and steal."

No one could translate Zwart's absurd lingua franca to know what he thought of the Delta's future. But Sutter was confident that the tulares would eventually be settled by American immigrant farmers. Briefly, he worried over a Hudson's Bay Company plan to secure a thirty-two square mile grant on the plains adjacent to the tule marshes, for a ranch to run a hundred thousand cattle and six thousand sheep. One *Californio* wrote the U.S. consul in Monterey, Thomas O. Larkin, that it was easy for the Mexican government to admit the Canadians into California but asked, rhetorically, "Will it be easy for the Government to drive them out?" He answered himself, *"Pienso que no!"* ("I think not!"). Luckily for the Americans, the settlement never advanced beyond the rumor stage.

The propagandist Lansford Hastings echoed Sutter in urging settlement of the Central Valley and countered the negative reports of Lt. Comdr. Charles Wilkes of the U.S. Navy's exploring expedition. In 1841, Wilkes dismissed Sutter's astonishing success and stated that the Valley was an area of inferior soils under water so long each year as to be unfit for settlement.

Wilkes was dead wrong. When his fellow officer, Commodore Cadwalader Ringgold, charted the Sacramento in 1849–50, he found several pockets of pre-emptors, both "gardeners" and woodcutters, already in the Delta. The claims of men named Todd, Matheny, McDonald, and Reuben ran along Grand Island's shore of the Sacramento's Middle Fork, as Ringgold termed Steamboat Slough, near Walker and Howard landings of later years. At the northernmost tip of Grand Island he found "Barber, Sr.," the patriarch of a clan that included a son farming across the river on the site of Courtland. Below him and two intervening rancherias were Armstead Runyon and his two sons. At Freeport, then called Webster's, or Russian, Embarcadero (for the Slavs who used to load Sutter's wheat there), he found another tiny settlement. (Earlier, Grimshaw had called it Tobias Kadell's [Cadell's?] Landing.)

The commodore, like Sutter and unlike Wilkes, was a visionary. He anticipated levee building and predicted that the Sacramento islands would be reclaimed for agriculture. "Doubtless, the inconvenience of annual overflow and inundation will be surmounted by the hardy settlers; this once accomplished, the soil—so very rich—will abundantly repay for all the toil bestowed." He predicted a thriving future for Rio Vista though, unaccountably, he confused it with Suisun City. He found few obstacles to navigation and none that could not be easily cleared. The river, still unpolluted by gold mining, ran crystal clear over a bed of clay and sand, as did beautiful Merritt Slough, today's Steamboat Slough. A year before the commodore, Grimshaw described it: "The branches of the large sycamores growing at the river's edge met and formed an almost continuous arch, overhead."

Ringgold was particularly impressed by the elder Barber, though he failed to record his Christian name. An octogenarian, at least, he was that rare bird in California, a Revolutionary War veteran. The commodore wrote: "Industrious citizens are constantly locating and taking up lands along the course of the river, in accordance with pre-emption rights. Among them I may mention a very respectable man, Barber, and his two sons. On both banks of the river at the formation of the Middle Fork they have cast their lot. . . . The father served under Washington at the Battle of Trenton and, although on the verge of four score years, he faithfully went through the campaigns in California during the Mexican War, his sons following his example."

Surprisingly, the squatter-farmers clung to their clearings throughout the winter floods of 1849–50 and the sickly season following. In San Francisco, Bayard Taylor described the "numbers of pale, emaciated frames, broken down by ague and diarrhoeas, [which] were daily arriving in the launches and steamers."

The only industry, of sorts, in the Delta besides vegetable gardening, the salmon fishery, and a bit of *aguardiente* ("brandy") making from wild grapes on the natural levees, was woodcutting. Trees were cut up not only to supply Sacramento, Stockton, and San Francisco with firewood, but also to make stockpiles of fuel for river steamers.

Ringgold noted that "a lively scene is presented to persons passing up and down the river; at almost every bend and turn, the woodcutter is seen and the pleasant sound of his axe heard, with hundreds of cords of wood convenient for transportation. Gardens, patches, and wider signs of cultivation greet the eye."

The eccentric George McDougal, later a "king of the cannibal islands" in Patagonia, and his egocentric brother, John ("I, John . . .") McDougal, later governor of California, tried to make Sutterville, below Sacramento City, into a logging port. In the May 19, 1849, *Placer Times*, they called for enough woodsmen to cut ten thousand cords of wood for the coming steamers. Probably not a stick was cut there.

The pioneers of the wood business were Joseph

Sims and Charles H. Ross, in the autumn of 1849, on a plot below Freeport, but their cabin and stacked logs were all swept away by floods. Like Ringgold, Bayard Taylor saw great woodpiles on "The Slough" (Steamboat Slough) in 1849, where steamers backed up to the banks to "wood up." The brothers who founded Antioch, via Smith's Landing in 1849, Joseph and W. W. Smith, got their start by cutting wood to supply the New York House, a hotel in the "paper" city of New York of the Pacific, now Pittsburg.

Hart F. Smith chopped wood in 1852–53 for two dollars a cord, before returning to farming on Grand Island. It was sold for twelve to fifteen dollars a cord to steamboats. Legrand R. Davis chopped wood for two years on a tract four miles below Georgiana Slough before he sold out in 1853. He bought the fastest boat on the river, the sixty-ton sloop *Bianca*, and hauled wood to the San Francisco market. James B. Welty was another who chopped wood. He worked for Clarkson C. Freeman all winter long in 1853–54 below Sutterville. After trying brickmaking, he returned that winter of 1854–55 for another year of axe work. Then he hired woodcutters and drove a team and wagon to supply his Sacramento woodyard.

A great Delta pioneer, Levi Painter, had to work as a woodcutter for four months at seventy-five dollars a month to make ends meet circa 1854–55, and another prominent farmer, Eben R. Parvin, chopped wood and cleared land in 1855 in order to be able to buy property on Grand Island in 1859. Unfortunately, he was paid in mortgages. The 1862 flood ruined their value and inac-

curate surveys forced him to buy parts of his 650-acre spread three times over—first from the alleged owner, then from the state, and finally from the federal government. But he stuck it out, and when the erstwhile woodcutter finally found himself holding clear title, he put 90 acres into orchards.

In 1880, the Oakland firm of Thompson & West published an exemplary "mugbook" history of Sacramento County. It was illustrated with many lithographic portraits of proud river pioneers and views of the chief subjects of their pride, extensive farms and ranches suggesting a lifestyle like that of the South's plantations.

Of the earliest birds noted by Ringgold, only Orin Randolph Runyon and his brother, Solomon, were among the Delta leaders of 1880. The former, a forty-niner born in Illinois in 1833, was given a very brief mention—"He is an extensive fruit grower." His brother's palatial farm, with its fine residence and formal garden—and the steamer *Pride of the River* moored at his landing—was featured as a double-page litho view, but Sol did not rate a biographical sketch.

The Runyons fared better in an 1890 county history by Winfield J. Davis. Their grandfather, Michael, and father, Armstead, came to California in 1849 to take up 160 acres below Courtland. They purchased more plots till the family had about a section of land and a mile of river frontage.

Orin worked for his father till 1855, when he left the state. He returned to fruit raising on his father's place in 1870. Two-thirds of the 300 acres of the home place were still in overflowed land, but Orin and his wife, Martha, kept the 100 improved acres in fruit trees and alfalfa.

Solomon, also a forty-niner born in Illinois, turned to farming in Solano County after two years in the gold mines. In 1859, he bought his own home place next to his father's ranch, later Orin's. Sol kept increasing the original 4 or 5 acres of orchards until he had 80 acres by 1890. In 1871 he bought 155 acres of land downriver at the head of Andrus Island, and ten years later, bought still more land to bring his total to 441 acres. The 200 acres in fruit made him one of the largest orchardists in the West. Although, like O.R., he had little chance for an education, he was a prominent Knight Templar, a director of the Sacramento Railway, and treasurer of the State Board of Horticulture.

To Winfield Davis, Solomon was an even greater paragon than most of the seemingly saintly founding fathers he eulogized in his "mugbook." "As may be judged, he is kept pretty busy superintending his various interests, but what is still better is that he is universally regarded by his neighbors as an entirely reliable upright man, a public-spirited citizen, kindly and obliging in his relations with his neighbors."

Of the ninety-eight persons whose lives were sketched in 1880, ten were from Ohio. New York supplied eight, Illinois, seven. There was one Swede, two Danes, the first of many Delta Portuguese (William Silva), and one Frenchman. William H. Barry (Irish?) was born in South America. A surprising eighteen of the select pioneers were Germans, doubtless the most assimilable of all immigrants.

The acreages of the agricultural elite varied from only 36 acres to a whopping 864 acres. The wealthiest man, Josiah Buckman Greene, held 114 acres on the Yolo shore opposite the upper end of Randall Island, plus a 750-acre ranch across the river in Sacramento County. His ten thousand choice trees—60 acres of pears, peaches, apricots, and cherries—were supplemented by 10 acres in vegetables. The balance was still in tules.

Greene had originally bought title—a squatter's quit claim—in 1850 to Merritt Island land near Clarksburg in Yolo County, for six hundred dollars. He took a steamer up the Sacramento to examine it, but the Delta was so flooded that he may have steamed right over his land. In Sacramento City he built himself a flatboat and drifted back downstream until, by "diligent inquiry," he located his property, still under several feet of water. He left his brother, Sylvester, and a friend in charge while he went to the mines to "make his pile." When he returned, he was astonished to find that his partners had done well, harvesting fifty tons of wild hay from bluegrass and clover, worth fifty dollars a ton. He began raising vegetables to haul to the Northern Mines.

In the fall of 1851, Greene began to protect his investment with one of the first island levees ever raised. He used his own hands and teams, reinforcing the piled-up soil with sycamore logs.

Greene's home was the first on the island. He made it an estate and a place of beauty. Though he was a very hard-working man, the devout New Englander always kept the Sabbath. Born in New Hampshire in 1818, he had been a successful jeweler in Virginia before changing careers and coming to California to farm. In his adopted state, he served as a levee commissioner and as a Yolo County Supervisor. He and his wife, Caroline, had four sons. When he died, in 1889, Greene was buried on his ranch in a spot that he loved. But, as is so often the case in the Delta, the river had the last word. The levee had to be raised and widened to protect the island, threatened again by flooding. His remains, and those of his wife, who died in 1898, had to be reburied in East Lawn Cemetery, Sacramento.

Josiah's son, George Buckman Greene, born in Virginia in 1849, was said to be the first white child to live on the Sacramento River below the city. He worked on his father's place first, then rented it, circa 1871, and finally bought it in 1886. A natural designer-inventor, Greene built his own steam launch and doubled as its skipper and engineer. Historian Davis termed the craft "the pride of this section." He served as a member of the Board of Swamp Land Trustees in District 150. Like his father, George Greene was a distinguished orchardist, with seven thousand trees.

Dwight Hollister, born in Ohio in 1824, came to California via Cape Horn in 1849. He mined for only a year, then went into agriculture in the area around Courtland and Richland (Hood). He used eighty acres for orchards and vineyards, the remainder for produce fields and pastures for his hundred-animal dairy herd. He had an "Honorable" tacked before his name because he not only served on the Sacramento Board of Supervisors but also served as an assemblyman in the state legislature. He and his wife, Nannie, were most proud, however, of his informal title—The Pioneer Fruit

Grower of California. This he earned by his early efforts to market pears. He was not the first to grow the fruit, by a long shot; the missionaries raised pears as early as 1792. But Hollister, in his various official capacities, became the earliest real spokesman for Delta horticulture. W. J. Davis said of him that "he was known among his associates as one true to the interests of his section, fearless in the expression of what he believed to be right, and tireless in his efforts in the direction of wise legislation."

Hollister's fellow Buckeye, Reuben Kercheval (born 1820), reached the Sacramento at about the same time. He located first on Ryer Island with his brother, Albert, but they soon took over (with their father, Louis) the north end of Grand Island, where Ringgold had earlier found the Revolutionary War vet, Barber. Reuben later bought out his brother's interest to become the owner of 330 acres. His chief claim to fame was in initiating levee building on the river.

The family continued Kercheval's dedication to the Delta after his death in 1881. The widow Kercheval managed the estate well, adding eighty-two acres to his original seventy of fruit trees during the decade of the eighties. She also carried on his heroic efforts to levee and reclaim all of Grand Island. According to Davis, "With untiring industry and business ability truly remarkable in a lady, Mrs. Kercheval is ever busily engaged in enlarging, improving and beautifying her landed possessions."

Reuben Kercheval's levee building was quickly imitated. By 1853, dikes (usually atop the natural levees) were protecting the Sacramento's east shore, parts of Merritt, upper Tyler, and Grand islands, and stretches along the Mokelumne and Calaveras rivers. These were low "shoestring" levees, often only a foot high, but they pointed the way for the massive embankments that were in place throughout the Delta by the century's end.

Indiana-born Levi Painter started west from his Missouri home in 1849 but stopped off on the Nebraska plains to become an Indian trader. He did not reach California till 1853. The ex-Hoosier, ex-Missourian "Pike" then worked for fifty dollars a month on the ranch he would shortly own. But after five months as a ranch hand, he crossed to the west side of the Sacramento to chop wood for four months at seventy-five dollars a month. In 1855 he went back to ranching on Sutter Island but, that December, settled for good on his 123 acres south of Courtland.

For ten years, Painter raised little but vegetables, then he ventured into the cattle and hog business. But the 1862 flood took two hundred of his animals. He never again took any interest in livestock, other than keeping a milch cow for the family. About 1865, Painter turned his attention to fruit growing. By 1889, he had thirty acres of orchards and forty of vineyards, while he continued tending his vegetable plots.

Levi Painter was one of a handful of Delta pioneers memorialized by place-names, like George Andrus of Andrus Island and Julius C. Beach, for whom intermittent Beach Lake, southeast of Freeport in the Sacramento Basin, is named. Painter divided up three and a quarter acres into building lots in 1879 and the hamlet-port of Paintersville grew up. It is recalled today by the Paintersville Bridge south of Courtland.

All of the Delta pioneers were self-made men—and women. Surprisingly for that day, when women were supposed to "know their place" (that is, the kitchen), the county historians singled out several ladies as leaders of the Delta farming community. Of course, they ran to widows of extinct male pioneers. Besides the widow Kercheval, there was Mrs. D. D. Gammon, Mrs. Louis Walthers, and Mrs. R. F. Davis. Most interesting was Robert Gourlie's wife. She was the widow Neubarer when the Scotsman met her. She came to Missouri from Germany in 1845, then to California in 1849. But she was barely three weeks on the plains before she had to dig a grave and bury her husband, a cholera victim. Friends urged her not to continue on, but she was a courageous woman and she reached Sacramento safely after 185 days of travel. She kept a boardinghouse so well that, besides supporting herself and her brood, she accumulated property, before marrying the Scot in 1854.

Not all Deltans made money hand over fist, at least at first. Myron Smith was badly hit by the 1862 flood and was apparently "land poor" in 1880. J. T. Arnold's experiment in farming the center of Grand Island in 1873 was a disaster. He was able to harvest but one of four crops he put into the ground before he moved to the island's margin to better his luck. Willard Hazen eventually became prosperous, but he lost his shirt in the 1862 flood that swept the Richland area. So blasted were his bright dreams that he did not feel ready to marry the patient Miss H. M. Eastman until sixteen years after their betrothal.

As folks grew financially well-off, they pulled down their old cabins and built cozy riverside cottages or bungalows. Some were erected by local contractors or carpenters from how-to-do-it books or catalogues of architectural styles, like Palladian manuals. Some were put together, *in situ*, of prefabricated parts shipped around the Horn to San Francisco. The new homes perched on protective berms — man-made mounds — or on stilts, with second stories to which families could flee from flood-invaded ground floors.

The wealthy, the nouveau riche "pearistocracy" and potato/asparagus barons, likewise tore down their old cabins. But they built great country houses in the ornate carpenter Gothic, or scrollsaw Gothic, style that Victorians loved. The structures might be hung with bay windows, topped with turrets, gables, and widow's walks, perhaps sheathed in fishscale shingles and trimmed with decorative elements borrowed from the opulent Queen Anne, Shingle, Italianate, and Eastlake architecture of San Francisco's Nob Hill.

All of the pioneer Deltans were inordinately proud of their fine homes, the necessary symbols of worldly success. The plates illustrating Thompson & West's *History of Sacramento County* showed not only pin-neat farms, ranches, and orchards, with sidewheelers and sternwheelers nuzzling up to the landings, but also the charming and palatial piles of architecture that passed for Delta farmhouses. The locals wished to demonstrate to the world that they were people of some

cultivation, not the rustics of tradition. Even the lone bachelor of Grand Island, Peter Hanson, lived in a ten-room house by 1866.

Landscaped grounds featured exotic ornamental shrubs, decorative citrus trees, rose gardens, camellias, oleanders, magnolias, and palms. Ancient fig trees, surviving from early horticultural and marketing experiments, were incorporated. For shade from the relentless summer sun, Deltans planted sycamores, walnuts, and eucalyptus along levee roads.

Perhaps Peter B. Green's career was typical of the area's upward social mobility. The German immigrant first worked on a farm in the rich Pearson District when Randall Island really was an island. The slough, later earth-filled, that marked its southern boundary ran twenty feet of water. He went to school in Walnut Grove in 1862 to perfect his English. After careers in mining and law "outside," he returned in 1871 to put together a productive fruit ranch with his wife, Cynthia. Their handsome, fourteen-room residence near Richland was described with shrinking violet modesty as "a very comfortable and elegant home."

The storybook woodcutter-who-made-good, Hart F. Smith, by 1878 had an imposing three-story home pictured in the 1880 mugbook history of Sacramento County, while George Thisby's widow kept up with the Joneses not only by erecting a two thousand dollar barn on her Georgiana Slough pear "estate," but by putting another four thousand dollars into improvements on the farmhouse that had succeeded her late husband's tiny original cabin. Reuben Kercheval's widow, Margaret, erected a handsome two-story house for her son Howard, a mile below the family mansion on Grand Island's head, and also a less pretentious structure (one story and a basement)—"but scarcely less elegant" (Davis)—for her son Hartley, on an eighty-two-acre parcel she bought.

Sol Runyon and his wife, Adaline, supplanted the old Runyon Place with one of the finest mansions on the river. His brother, Orin Randolph Runyon, built a beautiful sixty-foot square residence (1878) of which W. J. Davis observed, "It must have cost over $12,000 to build and finish, not to mention the additional outlay for interior ornamentation."

The residence of George B. and Alice Greene was described in a matter-of-fact manner as a pretty and well-designed two-story home, flanked by carefully kept grounds and neatly trimmed trees, but the Hon. Dwight Hollister's place was, in Davis's words, "one of the fair homes which industry and thrift has [sic] built up beside the soft-flowing Sacramento in this land of golden sunshine . . . the conspicuous landmark of a happy home not built, it is true, in a day, but the outcome of years of painstaking labor, a monument to a successful life."

Winfield Davis pulled out all the stops in singing the praises of the country seats of William H. Fry and Henry Cook. "The [Fry] home is a large, handsome structure, containing all the comforts and luxuries necessary to a rational enjoyment of life and thoroughly permeated with the wholesome intellectual and kindly spirit of both parents. . . . The residence of Mr. and Mrs. Cook is a very neat and commodious one, well supplied with the conveniences and comforts of a home, and with an exceptionally fine flower garden in front, exhibiting internally and externally the excellent taste of Mrs. Cook and her intimate compliance with that excellent commandment—'make home beautiful.' "

One of the most unusual homes was the large, two-story Painter's Hall, once the Paintersville meeting-house, for years the district's dance hall, and even, for a time, a salmon cannery bunkhouse. Levi Painter finished it in 1877 in time for the locality to celebrate that year's holiday with festivities in it. In the late eighties he moved it to the lower end of Paintersville, near his warehouse. He raised it up on a brick foundation and refitted it into a spacious residence for himself and his second wife, Maggie, whom he married in 1887. His first bride, Mary, died in 1867, leaving him three children.

The men and women of the Myers clan were interesting Delta folk. German-born (1834) Henry William Myers first arrived on Grand Island from his Ohio farm in 1857. He worked as a hand for $45 a month on a 250-acre ranch that he rented in 1864 and bought the next year. He raised vegetables and found that potatoes seemed to explode with growth in the rich soil. One 45-acre plot alone gave him eleven thousand 140-pound sacks of spuds. After eight months, he took a partner to buy, for $700, a place on Sutter Island which he worked for three years. About 1869, he switched from vegetables to fruit trees. By the 1880s, he had forty acres of orchards on Grand Island, plus a 120-acre ranch on

Miner Slough in Solano County. Unfortunately, in February of 1881 his home place was overflowed. But the levee was repaired in 1889 to make flooding a thing of the past, and his land, once again, was transformed into a garden spot. Before he was through, Henry and his wife, Sophia, had four children, Louis and Edward, Dora and Wilhelmina; 143 acres worth $10,725 (in 1890) in land and improvements; and a beautiful home, featured in a litho "view" illustrating their county's history.

Frederick Myers, born in Germany in 1822, came to Grand Island in 1866 as a wounded Civil War veteran. He bought seventy-six acres from his brother, though it was mostly a waste of tules and willows. He changed twenty acres into pear orchards and part of the balance into cropland by the century's last decade. W. J. Davis wrote of him: "He has a comfortable home and expects to become rich by the thorough reclamation of Grand Island."

Only a few of the Delta's great old homes have survived to suggest the quiet elegance of pastoral California of a half-century or a full century ago. Only one, State Senator William Johnston's Rosebud Farm, is protected by listing on the national register of historic sites.

The last-built of the truly great family seats was—and still is—the grandest of all. Henry Myers's comfortable 1876 eight-room house was small potatoes compared to his son Louis's classic Italianate mansion, though the latter was never completely finished. The grandiose, fifty-room, $350,000 River Mansion on Steamboat Slough boasts a ballroom, a theater, and a bowling alley. Myers, born in 1869, died in 1923 as his personal Bartlett pear empire was crumbling. The market collapsed after he turned field crop land into orchards—which had to wait for ten years before bearing a first harvest. The Pacific Fruit Exchange, which had fed the farmers' vanity by lending them money that enabled them to live in the grand manner—far beyond their means—foreclosed on Grand Island's big Smith and Myers ranches.

The pear crisis was accompanied by another blow to the genteel folk of the Delta, the wearing out of prime asparagus fields on the Sacramento after a dozen or fifteen years of intensive cropping. The fields lost their fertility and became diseased; the plants weakened and died. Sensible farmers who chose a modest style of life, and who hedged their bets with diversified crops, managed to hang on. Men like Myers, who lived dangerously, seeking a one-crop "killing" in the market, perished.

The Delta traditions of the pioneering Kerchevals, Greenes, and Runyons are continued today by such clans as the Darsie, Pettigrew, Van Loben Sels, Gwerder, Brooks, and Brown families. But the old elegance—indeed, opulence—is long gone. It is memorialized by the River Mansion, but that ornate palace on Steamboat Slough is a monument to a time that now seems as distant to us as that of Stonehenge.

Facing: the River Mansion

Interior, the River Mansion

Bank of Courtland

Joseph Gwerder home

Lester Greene home

Sol Runyon home

Drusella Gammon home

Pear orchard, April

Orchard ladders, the Besso place

Truck and shed

Residences, Locke

Isleton

Rooming house, Courtland

Levee steps, George Smith home

George Smith home
Overleaf: Pear orchard, December

DELTA PIONEERS FOUND ETERNAL VIGILANCE was the price of prosperity as well as liberty. They had to fight an endless battle with eroding, flooding rivers. Their only real weapon was Mother Earth—at least that portion that they could heap up into levees. And they could never predict where a beaver, gopher, or tiny, burrowing ground squirrel might undermine a dike. It was all a matter of chance, a "crapshoot" as the locals put it. They pointed with chagrin at the $350,000 spent on the west side of the Webb Tract, where all of the wind, tide, and wave action was concentrated—until a freak norther gnawed a hole in the northeast bank.

The long fight to reclaim the lowlands for agriculture began as a spinoff of Sacramento City's battle, with levees, against the flooding river in 1850. As early as 1849, Bayard Taylor had urged embankments for the Delta, predicting that agriculture would make it "one of the most beautiful and productive portions of the Union." During the 1850s, the lower Sacramento's east bank became a solid string of farms; the farmers, called rimlanders, built low levees atop the natural bank to protect their small holdings. A disconnected line of clearings lay on the opposite shore, and the tips of Sutter and Grand islands began to be tilled.

Among the earliest agriculturalists to heed Bayard Taylor was Reuben Kercheval. He began the first reclamation levee in 1850 on the tip of Grand Island. Kercheval raised it higher in 1851, but it went out, anyway. He then got a larger gang of Indians, kanakas, and especially, Chinese in 1853 to build a great wall of earth, three feet high, three feet across the crown, and

Part Four

Pears, Spuds, and Asparagus

thirteen feet at the base, for a dozen miles. He paid them 13½ cents a cubic yard for dirt moved by shovels and wheelbarrows. Time after time, Kercheval's exemplary and oft-strengthened levee failed, but he never lost faith; he always rebuilt it stronger. His neighbors tied into his levee and, by 1857, the apex of the island was protected by eighteen miles of dikes of various sizes.

Amazingly, Grand Island reclamation cost only a dollar an acre, at first. The flood of 1861–62 soon revised that figure. The ramparts built in 1868 to six feet brought reclamation costs up also, to five dollars an acre, and costs continued to climb as the height was raised again, by 1892, to eight feet, with some bases measuring thirty to forty feet, toe to toe. Costs dropped, of course, once efficient dredges were introduced to the Delta, late in the nineteenth century.

The first results of reclamation seemed miraculous. George McKinstry, Jr., wrote Edward Kern in 1851 of cabbages weighing fifty-three pounds a head and Irish potatoes measuring thirty-three inches in circumference. Small wonder that other lower Sacramento River agriculturalists followed Kercheval's lead as farms crept down to Howard Landing and leapfrogged to the Rio Vista sector of the mainland. Josiah B. Greene started a levee on Merritt Island before the flood of 1852, and in 1852 George Andrus was protecting the seven thousand–acre island named for him by hiring Chinese levee builders. By 1853, low "shoestring" levees gave partial protection to Merritt, upper Tyler, and northern Grand islands.

But the battle was only begun. Andrus Island began

its long fight with the river in 1852, but its complete reclamation would have to wait till 1889. There was uncoordinated levee work on Sutter Island long before its first reclamation district was formed in 1880, but not till 1896 did the isle enjoy good flood protection. Tyler Island, settled as early as 1852, had only its upper tip reclaimed as late as the end of the antebellum decade. As for ditches and canals, the first drainage canal in the Yolo Basin was not dug till 1864.

In the South Delta, the levee banks of the San Joaquin, Mokelumne, Calaveras, and Stanislaus rivers were occupied by 1852. Next year, James Crozier and W. L. Wright pioneered levee building in the area. They hired men to raise eighteen acres of the natural banks of Rough and Ready Island, where they had a market garden. Their reclamation work, dumping fill from carts to build a four-foot dike above the waterline, was said to cost fifteen hundred dollars an acre, at first. When they got the hang of it, reclamation costs dropped to six hundred dollars per acre.

Also in the South Delta, irregular, discontinuous ridges were shoveled up to protect Roberts and Union islands by 1857, and the San Joaquin's east bank south of French Camp in 1861. District 17, east of Roberts Island, eventually enclosed a polder, or tract, of 6,450 acres. But probably the best levees were only three or four feet high.

The Sacramento's lower, flood-prone islands were slow to be developed, though Robert Beasley farmed Sherman Island in 1855 and A. A. Krull was hauling potatoes and garden vegetables from Merritt Island to

Hangtown, or Placerville, by 1859 or 1860. Sherman Island, named for the U.S. Surveyor General of California, Sherman Day, did not get even modest dikes till about 1859. In the nineties, it was still being reclaimed, with only a small area under cultivation. Merritt Island was luckier. Its reclamation district was organized in 1862 and its levees completed in 1876. It has not flooded since 1893. In 1865, the San Francisco capitalist, B. F. Mauldin, began reclamation of Ryer Island, but it was aborted with only a half-dozen miles of levee built in the sixties. Reclamation was resumed in the 1880s and nineties, but Ryer was not safe until modern clamshell dredges were brought in to heap huge embankments in 1907.

By the opening of the Civil War decade, it was apparent to pioneers that rugged individualism was not the answer to complete reclamation. A secure future lay only in cooperation, sufficient capitalization, and above all, proper coordination of a *system* of levees to avoid weak links in the lines of defence. Dikes had to be continuous, as well as high and strong, to repel raging rivers. So it was that, from 1860 to 1930, most of the salvage of more than 350,000 acres was done by local reclamation districts. (Even so, some acreages flooded three or more times after initial reclamation. Only Randall Island has never been overflowed.)

By coincidence, another important factor in reclamation—mechanization—began to be felt at the same time. J. T. Bailey made history in 1865 by using some sort of machine to speed up the reclaiming of Staten Island. As Harold Gilliam has said, the Delta became the birthplace of agricultural technology, which has revolutionized American farming. By the 1920s, combines—combined harvesters and threshers—were in use, some pulled by twenty-eight to thirty-two mules, but others towed by the newfangled tractors that Benjamin Holt had invented in 1904 to replace the old steam traction engines. Besides these Caterpillar tractors, "cats" for short, new plows, discs, cultivators, subsoilers, and backhoes were placed in use. In the fluffy asparagus peatlands, which sometimes shook like Alaskan muskeg bogs, farm machinery was equipped with enormously broad wheels to keep it from sinking.

In 1878, land developer Gen. Henry M. Naglee realized that reclamation was too big a job for local jurisdictions. He petitioned the state legislature for help. Thanks to state, and later federal, support, the 30,000 reclaimed acres of 1878 jumped to 323,000 in 1910 and to a peak of 490,000 by World War II. By 1889, there were 110 miles of levees in Sacramento County's Georgiana Township alone.

It was also in 1878 that a State Engineer, William Hammond Hall, was appointed. He died a political death, but the office became the Commissioner of Public Works and was finally swallowed up by the State Department of Engineering. Besides recommending a state-controlled system of levees, Hall urged that debris dams be built in the foothills to protect Delta waterways from shoaling and farmlands from flooding because of hydraulic mining debris. Some dams were eventually built, but not until the damage was done and after Judge Lorenzo Sawyer's landmark decision of 1884 that virtually banned "hydraulicking." Governor George Perkins also tied mining debris problems to reclamation in a special message to the legislature. Some of Hall's ideas were rejected, like his scheme to close off the big bend of the Sacramento to make Steamboat Slough the main channel.

Public mass meetings and formation of a River Improvement and Drainage Association put pressure on a legislature reluctant to take action on engineering reports until the "Feds" should share costs. Washington was slow to admit that its navigational responsibilities extended to flood control and reclamation, though all were inextricably entwined in the Delta.

Slowly, cooperation came. Army Corps of Engineers reports of the 1880s and nineties shaped legislation. A California Debris Commission of 1893 was followed, just before World War I, by cost-sharing in the construction of two hydraulic dredgers to widen and deepen the Sacramento from its mouth to Cache Slough. This was the beginning of the so-called Minor Project, a part of a basin-wide flood control plan unimaginatively called the Major Project. The latter was finally adopted in 1917, after a delay of six years, at the same time that the Flood Control Act formally extended the national government's responsibility to that area, as well as to navigation.

Not all components of the Major Project, like massive levees towering to more than twenty feet at the head of Grand Island, were in place till 1949. But earlier, the old idea of a drain in the Yolo Basin, to relieve flood pressure on lower Sacramento River levees, became a reality in the Yolo Bypass.

To keep the Stockton Channel from silting up, in 1902–12 Congress authorized a new dike and a Mormon Slough–Calaveras River diversion ditch. After 1913, the federal government maintained a nine-foot navigational channel to Stockton, eighty-eight miles from San Francisco by water. In 1937, the channel was deepened to twenty-six feet and to fifty feet in 1950. The so-called Delta City was once more a true inland deepwater port.

The capital had to wait till after 1946, and Congress's authorization of the Sacramento River Deep Water Ship Channel, before its dreams of again becoming a seaport were more than pipedreams. By this time, its rival had forty miles of waterfront, including skyscraper grain elevators.

From about 1908 through the 1920s, reclamation districts maintained levees with about four feet of freeboard above the high water mark of the 1907 flood. However, some dikes were allowed to deteriorate, and they collapsed before high tides and floodwaters of 1908 and after. The response was to build still higher dikes, some up to thirty feet high and two hundred feet wide. These barriers, with the spoil banks left by channel dredges, created the man-made landscape of today's Delta.

In recent years, earthen barriers to saltwater penetration have been proposed, but such schemes as the Biemond and Reber plans were deemed less practical, by the state's planners for a Central Valley Project and California Water Plan, than the simple use of pressure of river flow to forestall salinization. However, the freshwater barrier has been weakened by the Delta

Cross Channel's funneling of water via the Mokelumne-San Joaquin to the Contra Costa Canal and the San Joaquin Valley's Delta-Mendota Canal.

By the 1860s, there was such a surplus of vegetables over subsistence needs and local sales that a brisk trade began with the cities. It was the reason for the reclamation of Rough and Ready Island, for one. By 1861, the rich black loam and the sandy loam were found to be so amenable to double-cropping (two harvests a year from the same plot) that a Tyler Island farm, only half-rescued from tules, sold for six thousand dollars. In 1869, Chinese lessees were turning the natural levees on the river side of Roberts Island into long strips of truck and fruit gardens. Eight years later, a string of onion, bean, and blackberry plots reached Rough and Ready Island and spilled over into the old Pescadero Grant.

But the big news of the 1870s was the Delta's harvest of small grains. Both wheat and barley ran from a third to two-thirds higher in yield there than on the plains. That meant a harvest of two tons per acre. The reclaimed Delta was now called San Francisco's Bread Basket. When the wheat boom faded, it came to be called The Garden District of California.

Besides grain and the "trademark" crops that made the Delta world-famous—Bartlett pears, asparagus, and Irish potatoes—the land has proven ideal for tomatoes, sweet corn and field corn, beans, melons, squash, sweet potatoes, onions, sugar beets, apricots, peaches, celery, and alfalfa. Less rewarding were experiments with peanuts, rice, jute, ramie, hemp, cranberries, mulberries, peppermint, and spearmint. Pomelos, Chinese grapefruit, were tried, and the federal government experimented with sugar cane (1894–95) on Union Island and the Terminous Tract. Chicory was hardly a wild success, but it was not the soil's fault. It was grown on Roberts Island and in Reclamation District 17, 1860–1914, and there was a factory in Stockton. But San Francisco's coffee roasters could not convert their customers' taste to the continental brew.

At first, settlers cleared peat land by burning off the tules, but all-peat soils smouldered right down to the water table and this wasteful practice was stopped. Burning increased wind erosion, too. From a quarter to a half inch of top soil could be lost each year. Subsidence, accelerated by burning as well as by oxidation and compaction, was destructive of cropland. Ashy dust storms whirled into settlements. The costs of ditching and pumping grew so large that sinking areas, like Franks Tract, had to be abandoned by agriculturalists to yachtsmen, houseboaters, fishermen, and the "miners" of peat for gardens.

In great contrast to the disaster of Franks Tract was the rescue of the Pearson District around Courtland. In 1878 the levee gave way and the back country became a lake. So badly hurt were the ranchers that the San Francisco Savings Union found itself the surprised owner of 4,000 acres of submerged land. P. J. Van Loben Sels supervised construction of a great second line of defense. It lay three and a half miles behind the riverside levee and its half-mile-wide belt of Bartletts. This pear paradise extended from Dwight Hollister's place to the W. E. Eastman ranch. The new dike, twenty-three feet high and twelve across at the crown, protected 9,000 acres. The Union paid half of the

$180,000 of this walling-off, and the pumping plant ate up $130,000 more. But, by 1889, every acre was ready for cultivation and many were already renting for $14 to $20 a year. When the lake in the lowest part of the district dried up in June, it became a field of beans that produced forty sacks to the acre in September.

Alex Brown, in 1887, leased 3,830 acres still held by the Union and raised two crops a year on what W. J. Davis called the "no longer Dismal Swamp." A 32-acre parcel yielded, in one year, 11,580 sacks of potatoes, 300 of onions, and 50 of sweet potatoes, plus a ton and a half of beans per acre. These yields made the Pearson District, in Davis's words, "a new Land of Goshen." By 1889, three new orchards were planted, the Union put up neat and substantial residences and barns for workers and subtenants, and Alex Brown was giving asparagus a try.

A promotional brochure of 1914 was being modest, not boastful, when it described Delta yields as always bountiful and usually phenomenal. It pointed to crop values of $100 to $200 per acre of asparagus (on 20,500 acres), $100 to $400 for pears, and $50 to $100 for potatoes. Almost seventy years ago, Delta fields— whatever the crop—were averaging out at $100 an acre in yield.

In recent years, there has been a shift from such distinctively Deltan crops as pears, potatoes, and asparagus to such mundane crops as field corn, alfalfa, sugar beets, and tomatoes. Today, California produces 80 percent of the nation's canning tomatoes, much of it from the Delta. The five million ton crop of 1981 was gathered not by big crews but by UC-Blackwelder harvesters, called "job eaters" by worried critics. These monsters, worth $160,000 each, lumber through the fields at only six miles per hour, but gather in a thousand pounds of ripe tomatoes each minute. No wonder that the Delta's new worry is overproduction and glutting of the market.

Horace ("Go West, Young Man . . .") Greeley was right more than once. He also said (in 1859), "Fruit growing is destined to be the ultimate glory of California." The levee corridor from Freeport to Iselton was already growing peaches, apples, nectarines, plums, and even quinces and figs, as Greeley took pen in hand. But pears triumphed over all rivals. The others simply could not handle the seepage and high water table; they disliked "wet feet." Bartlett pears spread from the east bank to Roberts, Union, Grand, Andrus, and Tyler islands, with sheds being thrown up alongside steamer landings.

Fruit was dried and transported by sea till completion of the transcontinental railroad in 1869. In 1870, 70 cars of fresh fruit were shipped east. It was 115 cars the next year, mostly pears. By 1876, New York and Chicago commission houses were sending purchasing agents into the Delta by riverboat. When "reefers," refrigerated railroad cars, were introduced, the market blossomed.

As early as 1878, owners were offered $1,000 an acre for prime orchard land, though the average price was below that as late as the 1920s. During the decade of the 1870s, a 640-acre farm near Courtland grossed between $5,000 and $10,000 a year from its 60 acres of pears, while only earning a total of $3,000 from all of its other products—butter, beef, and alfalfa seed.

The Bartlett, or "summer pear" (it is the first to ripen), was a European immigrant, like so many Delta agriculturalists themselves. It is the Williams pear of England, circa 1770, renamed in Massachusetts. But it found its true and perfect home in the Delta, where it brought wealth to many families because the species adapted itself so well to poorly drained land.

The great horticultural authority, Professor E. J. Wickson, wrote that the Bartlett not only defied excess moisture but "delighted" in soils at which other deciduous fruits would rebel. It withstood neglect as well as thrips, blights, and smuts. Wickson added, "Neither frost nor standing water can avail against it."

The romantic Wickson preferred the peach to the pear because of the former's "dash and spirit." But he considered the Bartlett to be one of California's most profitable fruits, fresh or canned. With its long (July–October), slow-ripening season—in some orchards there were two distinct crops—it was ideal for marketing. It was universally favored for shipping because it not only "carried" well without bruising or spoiling, but ripened during travel.

But the experts slighted the real reason for the Bartlett Boom in the Delta, the eager acceptance of the fruit by consumers. This was partly because of its size (a huge specimen of 1870 weighed in at four pounds, nine ounces) and its beauty. But its sweet aroma and rich flavor were more important than size and color. Wickson was right when he wrote, "The Bartlett is not only the greatest pear in California, but the greatest pear in the world."

In 1914, Wickson estimated that California's 1,751,326 already-bearing trees, of a total of 2,101,236 rooted, were producing 53,483 tons of pears a year. They commanded top prices in the London market, even besting peaches.

Around World War I, the Bartlett Boom peaked. The state produced 48½ percent of all American pears, and most of that figure belonged to the Delta. About 30 percent of the crop was canned, 50 percent sold fresh, and 20 percent—mostly windfalls—dried. Even the latter brought $35 a ton to the growers, while the overall average was $73. Choice canning fruit was worth a hefty $85 and the contents of the 4,300-plus railroad cars that pulled out of Sacramento in 1919 for the East were auctioned off at $90 to $100 a ton. Early choice Bartletts in dessert-hungry New York City were worth $6.20 a box. By 1923, pear orchards were averaging $250 to $400 an acre and some were producing $800, even $1,200.

Pears are still picked by hand, with skilled Chinese- and Japanese-Americans preferred. Pay can be either by the hour or by the piece, but dedicated orchardists will tell you that the fruit will be hurt unless pickers are hired by the hour. In such a case, "they will be kind to the Bartletts." The first pears are sent eastward by late June; the crop from later in the season is trucked to canneries or to cold storage in the cities.

Traditionally, pear orchards averaged fifty acres

and were owner operated, though there was some share-cropping, and a few were run for absentee landlords. Most pear growers have been Caucasians, with Asian work crews. An exception to the rule is Lincoln Chan, a Chinese-American of Courtland. Mr. Chan today has a thousand acres (mostly leased) in Bartletts, running from Sacramento's Metropolitan Airport to Walnut Grove.

Pears declined in importance as newly reclaimed lands were opened up, particularly for another bonanza crop—asparagus. The 16,500 acres of pears of 1929 shrank to 4,900 by 1945, before gradually leveling off. By the 1950s, there were some new, modest plantings. Nowadays, pear orchards are irrigated only two to four times a year. This is not only a laborsaving technique, it is ecologically sound. It extends the lives of the trees by not raising the water table and by not hastening the accumulation of salts as, unfortunately, frequent sub-irrigation and check irrigation used to do.

Some anonymous settlers on forty acres of river-bank south of Sacramento introduced asparagus to the Delta in the early 1850s. But the first shipments of "sparrow grass," or just "grass," were from Stockton, and not till 1880. By 1894, however, Sacramento River growers were netting, not grossing, $100 to $175 an acre from this most profitable of fresh vegetables. The Capital Packing Company had begun canning operations in 1882, but a later improvement in the process led to an explosion in sales. Asparagus became practically synonymous with the Delta. It was called the area's Prima Donna Crop when, by the 1900s, the greatest beds in the world there produced an $11,000,000 harvest, one-half of all produced in the United States.

Robert Hickmott planted a cannery as well as asparagus on Bouldin Island in 1892. In just four years, he was shipping carload lots and, by 1900, building a second packing plant. At the century's end, he had half of his six thousand Bouldin Island acres in the new crop. In 1901 his cannery was operating from mid-March to mid-June, putting twenty tons of spears into tins each day.

A rival cannery appeared on Bouldin Island in 1903, and that year, the two of them put up 100,000 cases, for which the world's epicures paid a neat half-million dollars. Asparagus rows and canneries spread to Grand, Andrus, and Jersey islands, and even invaded the Pearson pear paradise (a cannery was set up at Vorden, or Trask's Landing).

Around 1915, about two-thirds of this leading winter vegetable field crop was canned, in 1,031,269 cases. This amounted to 47,747,755 pounds, as contrasted with only 15,915,918 pounds in consignments of fresh asparagus.

Large commercial "plantations" spread through the Delta, since the asparagus plants grow readily from seed and set out new shoots annually. The soft peat soil was ridged up over the root crowns to produce the much-desired white stalks that were a virtual trademark of the Delta's canned spears. Fresh asparagus was usually not blanched, but left in its normal chlorophyllic garb.

The shoots were cut from mid-February to June or

July with a long butcher knife or a long-handled gouge. Then the plants were allowed to rest, to "go to fern." Stalks were graded and bunched for marketing, tied with cotton tape or raffia, and stood on end so as not to get the bends. The ends were cut off, and the bunches wrapped in oiled paper and packed in crates with a couple of inches of wet moss at the bottom to keep them moist, and an inch or two of space at the top of the crate. This was because, like fingernails, they continued to grow on their journeys and needed headroom.

A scare was thrown into the fields in 1905 when asparagus rust reached the Delta. But the U.C. Experiment Station and Professor R. E. Smith found that it could be controlled by using sulphur to protect the top growth after cutting. However, a real curse came to stay—Fusarium wilt. "Grass" can be counted on for a normal six to ten years of heavy yield and a total commercial life of a dozen years. But replanting is almost impossible because of the wilt.

As early as 1902, asparagus raising was a boom business. The twenty-dollar-a-ton price for it as fresh produce jumped to sixty dollars. Asparagus followed potatoes to the South Delta as land "wore out" on the Sacramento. At first it did not do well there, but then improved between 1909 and 1915. Canneries were soon found at Middle River, Orwood, Holt, and Antioch as well as in Stockton.

Most really productive areas of asparagus were still on the Sacramento when production hit 27,750,000 pounds in 1909–10. But, by 1924, the old fields of Grand, Andrus, Bouldin, Twitchell, and Jersey islands and the Pearson District of the mainland were all past their prime. Ryer Island followed them into defeat, then the Egbert District, and "grass" migrated from tiring soils to new plantings in the Yolo Basin and on Union, Coney, and Lower Roberts islands.

World War II saw a shift of "sparrow grass" to mineral lands, as well as disease-free new peat lands. The shift to nonpeat soils, by great luck, came just at a time of changing taste, when the blanching by the heaped-up peat was no longer necessary to please buyers.

An overall decline in asparagus set in and the crop almost disappeared from the Sacramento River. Canneries in Walnut Grove, Rio Vista, and Isleton dropped from ten in 1936 to none in 1950. After about 1952, Jersey and Bradford islands and the Webb Tract had to give up, and the crop barely held on at Staten and Bouldin islands. But Union, Victoria, and Lower Roberts islands, and the Fabian, Clifton Court, Byron, Wright, and Shima tracts on the mainland became preeminent. The San Joaquin area, which had held but 16 percent of the plantings of 1924, held 95 percent by 1952. Asparagus then occupied about 15 to 22 percent of all South Delta farmland.

Labor requirements are high in asparagus growing. The gangs of Japanese, Chinese, and some Hindus are gone, and most of the Filipinos too, replaced by Mexicans. But it remains an important production. The Bank of America reported an actual increase in acreage between 1979 and 1980, from 26,400 to 27,900 acres. Early season stalks are air-expressed to asparagus lovers in the East, followed by bulk shipments by rail within eight to twelve hours after cutting. In mid-April a shift occurs, and the crop is trucked to packers in nearby cities.

Surely, George Shima's is the great success story of the Delta. The potato was one of the area's first crops, grown with onions and cabbages in miserable clearings among the tules for sale to Sierra miners hopeful of a dietetic cure for scurvy when citrus was unavailable. Shima moved the humble Irish "pratie" from the garden patch to vast fields and made it big, big Delta business.

Shima was a young immigrant who had trained at an agricultural school in Japan, but when he began working in the Delta it was as a day laborer for tule farmer Arthur Thornton of New Hope. Thornton is named for him, the Shima Tract for his employee. Soon, Shima was farming a ten-acre plot on shares. He was very shrewd in business matters. By 1906–07, he had cornered the potato market in the Delta. He was soon being called California's Potato King. By 1910, he owned only 420 acres but leased an amazing 8,300 more. And in those days, Delta fields gave up four hundred bushels an acre.

Shima bought 1,500 acres of King Island and spent $75,000 on reclamation just before the Alien Land Law of 1913 went into effect to forbid the ownership of property by alien Orientals. In 1916 he leased another 25,000 acres, including Bacon Island, and in 1922 was still operating more than 12,000 acres, though the "pertater" boom was now over.

George Shima held stock in a firm founded by local and Oakland capital in 1907, the California Delta Farms Company. It was reminiscent of such great development companies ("land grabbers," cried their opponents) as the Glasgow-California Reclamation Company and George D. Roberts's Tide Lands Reclamation Company. The company was formed to develop the Webb, Holland, Orwood, and Empire tracts and King and Medford islands. For John Herd, Shima's firm leveed Mandeville and Bacon islands and the Shima, McDonald, Henning, and other tracts. Reclaiming was supervised by Lee Phillips, who had only an oral contract with Shima to obtain unreclaimed land, to levee it, and to turn it over to the Issei for clearing and potato planting.

Leases cost Shima $17 an acre the first year and $30 for the next two years. He then would have to move to fresh land because he was limited to three years' occupation by the hostile Alien Land Law. Happily for him, the term coincided exactly with the period of grace extended by Mother Nature before she allowed fungus to enter, and ruin, a productive potato patch.

The Japanese-American paid well for his leases of new land, but prospered by his sale of the 35 to 40 percent of each crop of spuds that he received from subleases to Japanese, Chinese, Hindu, and Italian farmers. A typical 1916 contract involved a lease of 2,700 acres of the Henning Tract for potatoes and onions at $20 an acre from Weyl-Zuckerman Company. He then subleased the acreage for $27.50, but furnished seed, some cash, and a foreman or overseer for the gangs of Japanese or Chinese workers. By 1915, 75 percent of all tenant farmers were Orientals. Field hands could each take care of seventy-five acres until digging time, when extra laborers were needed.

In 1918, Shima organized his Empire Navigation Company to manage his holdings, collect his share of crops, and buy and sell his potatoes and onions. He soon had his own fleet of towboats, barges, and gasoline launches to transport his root crops to San Francisco. The wheelhouse of one of his vessels is preserved today as an exhibit on the Hyde Street Wharf of San Francisco's National Maritime Museum.

The year's two potato crops were usually sold in the ground, well before harvesting time. They brought from thirty cents to three dollars a sack, but averaged one dollar. Gunnysack loads were hauled to landings to be picked up by steamboat-freighters or barges for the wholesale produce buyers of San Francisco, Sacramento, and Stockton.

Shima was not only the Delta's first great potato wholesaler, he was the first grower or shipper to adopt a trademark (his red sacks) and to carefully wash and grade his tubers before sacking them. He thus pioneered product standards, or quality control.

Shima learned that peat soils produced light-skinned potatoes. The Early Rose and American Wonder, early favorites, he replaced with the Burbank about 1894. It was later joined by the White Rose variety. With the application of commercial fertilizer, a single Delta area could produce 350 bushels of superb spuds.

A decline in potato culture followed World War I as labor, fertilizer, and farm machinery costs increased and the yield dropped to an average 155 bushels an acre. Still, 95 percent of California's commercial shipment of 6,200 railroad cars in 1919 came from Delta rows. And in the 1920s, when the California Delta Potato Growers Association was doing business at 833 Market in 'Frisco, it is said that ten million pounds of potatoes were still being dug in Delta fields each month.

By 1924, only 7 percent of the Delta's crop total was in potatoes, barely 1.8 percent in 1952. The last strongholds are McDonald and Bacon islands. Such Stockton names as Zuckerman and Weston have continued the grand old tradition of Delta spuds since Shima's day.

The development of large-scale agriculture in the Delta had its roots in the success of men like Shima. The farming of land in the interior Delta began with the Swamp Land Act of 1850, in which the federal government ceded overflowed lands to the state of California for sale to individuals. The surveyor general planned marsh drainage and the legislature implemented plans by authorizing land reclamation for agriculture (1851) and its sale (1855, 1858) by surveys. A 320-acre limit was dropped in 1868 when reclamation was returned from a (terminated) State Board of Reclamation Commissioners to the counties. Sacramento River ranches grew larger, but they were dwarfed by the family-run or corporate-owned holdings of the San Joaquin.

The Tide Lands Reclamation Company, 1869, was the greatest of its breed. Its George D. Roberts became the most successful land agent in the history of the West. The company was bought in 1879 by two large-scale Union Island developers, David Bixler and Gen.

Thomas H. Williams, the so-called Land Hog. Adjoining them on the old Pescadero properties was Gen. Henry M. Naglee. Other capitalist-investors and developers included M. C. Fisher, James Ben Ali Haggin, Lloyd Tevis, and Ross C. Sargent. California's agribusiness, seemingly running amok today in the grape and cotton fields of the southern San Joaquin Valley, alas, had its birth—like Moses—in the bulrushes of the San Joaquin's sleepy bayous.

The big outfits were a mixed blessing. They did, indeed, hog land. But they also had enough money to build proper levees. When the Land Hog General rebuilt almost fifty miles of Union Island's ramparts, he paid a thousand Chinese fifteen cents a cubic yard of dirt to create fields that would soon yield 26.6 bushels of wheat, grossing thirty-two dollars and netting seventeen dollars per acre. When Roberts teamed up with Williams in reclamation in 1877, they added teams and gangplows and eighty-two horse-drawn Fresno scrapers to a small army (three thousand) of Chinese. Then they really went modern and hired Col. Alexis Von Schmidt to build the first of a long line of dredges, starting with *Hercules* and *Thor*.

The Delta's story is not just one of reclamation and agriculture. Transportation and town settlement have been important factors, too. Sutter's little schooner had the region all to herself at first; though a tiny teakettle of a steamer, the *Sitka* (or *Little Sitka*) made it to New Helvetia, just once, in 1847, before being eviscerated of boiler and engine after she foundered. She was so slow that an ox team beat her from Benicia to Sutter's Fort.

The Gold Rush brought scores of sailing vessels and steamers—sidewheelers, sternwheelers, and "propellors"—to the rivers. By the end of 1850, twenty-eight steamers and many more sailing craft had made it to Sacramento. The early steamboats burned four-foot lengths of wood, about a cord (twelve dollars) an hour. Oak was preferred to cottonwood; bull pine was best of all. They switched to the low-grade coal dug from Mount Diablo and bunkered at Black Diamond (Pittsburg), before converting to oil at the century's turn.

Sailing vessels had a difficult time in the twisting rivers. Contrary winds (or none at all) combined with tides and currents so that it was often necessary to warp or kedge, to tow, even to cordelle—haul by a line of men on a makeshift towpath on the levee's crown. But even vessels like the big 241-ton, deep-draft, square-rigged bark *Whiton* made it safely to Sutter's Embarcadero before the river silted up and shoaled.

In only a few years after the gold discovery, some of America's finest steamboats were on the Sacramento. (The San Joaquin run was never as popular or important.) The *Senator* established regular passenger service in 1849, charging thirty dollars for a passage. Competition brought on a rate war and the price of a ticket went down to a dollar, four bits, a dime. (Some say that, for a spell, in a later fare war between the California Steam Navigation Company and its opposition, not only was passage free, but the company paid passengers to take its boats.) Rates later settled down to ten dollars to Sacramento from San Francisco, eight dollars to Stockton.

The *McKim* was the first of the newfangled "propellors" or screw steamers on the Delta. Her rival, the *Antelope,* which carried the first Pony Express mail in 1860, hauled so much Wells, Fargo & Company treasure that she was dubbed the Gold Boat. The *New World,* "kidnapped" by her master, Capt. Ned Wakeman, from a New York sheriff's sale, was famous on the river not only for her calliope and her cuisine, but her speed. She set an 1850s record on the San Francisco–Sacramento run via Steamboat Slough, but it was broken in 1861 by the classiest of all the riverboats, the *Chrysopolis,* nicknamed the "Chrissie," and titled the Queen of the River and the Slim Princess. Her record, for steam, stands to this day—five hours and nineteen minutes.

The thousand-passenger *Chrysopolis* featured not only a band but elegant cabins and murals. The *Senator* was proud of its rosewood staterooms and its four bridal suites. The opposition, independent boat *Defender* also had a band, though rival steamers would blow their whistles to drown it out when they could. Another opposition boat, the *Defiance,* brought the first calliope to the river in 1860. The later *Fort Sutter* and *Capital City* bragged of their staterooms—with baths!

Rivalry between boats was keen and races were common, but the Delta was lucky. There were collisions, sinkings, and explosions, but few considering the great volume of waterborne traffic. And in the long history of Delta steamboating there were only two major disasters in which the loss of life was large enough to cause conflicting totals in various reports. The opposition steamer *Washoe* blew up on a moonless night (September 5, 1864) near the mouth of Steamboat Slough as her captain, G. W. Kidd, tried to overtake the speeding *Chrysopolis.* An hour later, Capt. Albert Foster's *Antelope* picked up survivors from the burning boat. The *Union* of September 7 suggested the feeling of horror held by Sacramentans: "The *Washoe* tragedy is appalling . . . a stunning shock—a crash—the boat is a wreck. The dead, scarcely to be recognized, strew the splintered planks, the maimed and scalded are crying or moaning for help. . . . Then the long agony of waiting for succor, which comes at last as the *Antelope*'s lights shine over the dark waters."

On October 12, 1865, the *Washoe*'s California Steam Navigation Company rival, *Yosemite,* "blew" just as Captain Poole swung her away from the wharf at Rio Vista. Many of the dead, mostly scalded, were nameless Chinese workers crammed into the forward, below-decks steerage called the China hold. The *Chrysopolis* made the rescue. The coroner's jury blamed the "soft iron" of the *Yosemite*'s boilers.

Sailing craft and steamers alike had to fight a running, and ultimately, losing battle with the silting of the rivers by hydraulic mining in the Sierra. Deepwater vessels began to give up both rivers as early as 1866. Finally, high tides could no longer carry even the light-draft sternwheelers over Hog's Back Shoal in Steamboat Slough and, circa 1874–76, that shortcut was abandoned.

As early as 1854, Gen. A. A. Redington and Samuel J. Hensley formed the California Steam Navigation Company. It was independent, but monopolistic, till

1869, when it was taken over by the Central Pacific Railroad, later the Southern Pacific "Octopus." It then became even more monopolistic. Local farmers fought back by buying their own produce schooners, like the *Northern Lights* and the *Emma Adeline.*

In 1875, the local farmers formed a rival California Transportation Company with the sternwheeler *Reform* as its flagship. Unlike the snooty packets, unwilling to stop anywhere in the Delta but Rio Vista, and possibly Courtland, the farmers' own boats would stop anywhere, almost, at the wave of a flag by day or a lantern by night. (Jerry MacMullen wrote that they would pull over for a single lug of peaches.) Of course, the fiercely competitive CSNC boats did likewise. They zigzagged dizzily down the Sacramento, touching at dozens of two-bit landings. Probably the *Isleton* set a record in the 1890s when she made forty-six stops upward bound and seventy-six on her way back to San Francisco.

By the 1890s, the independents were forced off the Sacramento by the CSNC and off the San Joaquin by the California Navigation and Improvement Company. A last-ditch attempt to throw off the monopoly was made after 1900 when the farmers manned a mosquito fleet of gasoline-powered screw launches, towboats, and barges. In time, they switched to diesel fuel, but gave up the ghost when paved roads in the 1920s brought cheaper trucking to the Delta. (It was cheaper to ship by truck than boat because of much reduced cargo handling.)

By the end of the 1850s, thousands and thousands of people had seen the Delta. But only a tiny percentage ever set foot in it. However, a handful of the latter began to build steamboat landings, and some of them grew into towns. The riverboats and the landings lived a symbiotic existence; each depended on the other for life. The little wharves or brush-cushioned bank landings provided the necessary business in freight and passengers for the boats. The latter fed the tiny settlements with visitors, new citizens, freight, food, mail, clothing picked from Sears Roebuck and "Monkey" Ward catalogues, and theatrical troupes or musical groups to play rude meeting halls or even town squares. A few ladies of the night just might disembark around payday.

The riverboats were the links that tied Delta residents to the outside world. The boats' calls were social events. Whole towns rushed to the wharves to see who was a'comin' visiting, while Chinese, Japanese, and turbaned Sikhs trooped ashore, almost unnoticed. Here one picked up news, gossip, and rumors—and snooped to see who was off to the City on a spree.

There were all kinds of craft in the Delta trade, including fruit and vegetable schooners and scows, "spud boats" for potatoes (like the *Mandeville,* a derelict in the tules today), general store boats that traded merchandise for either cash or produce, and Chinatown boats that brought up singsong girls from *Dupont Gai* (Grant Avenue), and *fan tan* and *pai gow* tables for gaming.

The steamboat whistles were as distinctive as trademarks, as easily recognized by locals as the melodious steam calliopes of some boats. In the daytime, at the first blast of a distant whistle, excited kids would shinny up tall trees or scramble up windmill towers to be the first to shout word of smoke, visible perhaps a mile away. If it was the *Whipple*, Dick and Marie Phipps recalled for Steve Simmons, there would be a holler—"Give us a tune!" And the calliope would steam into action.

When local families visited San Francisco, they would often take the *Delta Queen* down as a "sleeper," spend the day in town, and return the next night, on the *Delta King*. Naturally, school chums would be alerted to welcome the kids back with yells and screams—to the obvious embarrassment of parents.

The steamboat whistles were not just for entertaining river people. Nor just to alert dock wallopers to make wharves and warehouses ready. They would warn off approaching vessels and bounce their blasts off riverbanks, buildings, and special echo boards set up on the levees for skippers and pilots to feel their way when blinded by tule fog or darkness.

Of the many landings, barely a handful are towns today. Some were swept away by floods, like Rio Vista (number one), Emmaton, and Mokelumne City. Montezuma languished for lack of timber for building materials. Bidwell's Brazorians were starved out.

The Mormons who founded New Hope on the north bank of the Stanislaus River near its mouth started out very well. They sowed an acreage of wheat and erected log cabins and a sawmill. But the Saints had to abandon their colony when it was wracked—and then wrecked—by dissension. An attempt to revive it as Stanislaus City failed. Edwin Bryant reported only two

or three houses left in 1849. Today it is remembered because of the popular boating marina west of Thornton—New Hope Landing.

Staten Island's Hagginsville memorialized entrepreneur James Ben Ali Haggin, but it yielded to its rival Walnut Grove around 1879. Onisbo, a mile or two south of Courtland, was named by Armstead Runyon for his friend, a local Indian chief who died on Runyon's ranch on October 24, 1862. The corpse of the well-liked ninety-year-old was not given to his people to be ceremoniously burnt. Instead, his body was given a Christian-style funeral and burial. The town called it quits in 1868 when its post office was transferred to Courtland.

Collinsville, the old Italian commercial fishing port with its houses high on stilts, is moribund. Nearby Toland's Landing is dead and gone. The landing where W. W. Brison shipped Vaca Valley wheat on the *Ohio* for Sacramento in 1851 became the busy little grain port of Maine Prairie in 1854, its founder a Captain Merrithew. The Cache Creek port's 50,000 tons was second only to Stockton's in 1863. But it succumbed, as did Denverton, named for the James W. Denver of Colorado's capital, to the railroad stops of Dixon and Elmira.

Suisun City, still very much with us, began when farmer Daniel Berry arrived on the site in 1848. The first vessel to call there was Captain Wing's schooner *Ann Sophia* in 1851, and by the next year, loads of potatoes were being shipped out of the tiny port.

Venice, on the island of the same name, died as a result of a bad hunch. Its speculators in the late 1860s guessed that mining debris would clog the Stockton Channel and force a transfer of the grain trade to their new port. In 1871, a single house stood there as a monument to the scheme.

Brach's Landing suffered a crib death, but is recalled by today's (misspelled) Brack Tract. Moore's Landing on Old River gave up the ghost when gandy dancers spiked-in Bethany's railroad siding in 1868. Banta saved itself only by moving bodily to the railroad.

Freeport was born a railroad town in 1862, the terminal of a short line in opposition to the Sacramento Valley Railroad and the high fees charged at Sacramento's Embarcadero. The town grew to about four hundred, as ten miles of road were built before the Central Pacific bought up the nuisance line. Besides a sugar beet loading dump and a gas pump and saloon to serve sportsmen using the dock near an important Sacramento River bridge, Freeport is famous for A. J. Bump's restaurant.

Vorden, or Trask's Landing, died when its post office was moved to Locke. Bryan's Landing and Richland are long gone. Paintersville succumbed when steamers would no longer call there. The bascule Paintersville Bridge recalls Levi Painter and his Post Hole Bank. He used to hide his money, by night, under a particular, memorized fence post. (Dennis Leary of Grand Island had a similar savings institution—his Sycamore Tree Bank. He stashed his cash in a hole in a bole of a sycamore, sealing it up after every deposit.)

Antioch flourishes today and guards the southern entry into the Delta, the Nejedly high-rise bridge, built since the old (1926) Antioch Bridge was dismantled after being rammed too many times—1958, 1963, 1970. New York of the Pacific and Black Diamond have reincarnated in Pittsburg. Rio Vista, "Rye-o Visty," to some old-timers, remains important. For years, it was the only Delta port-of-call of the Sacramento packets. All of the region's trade funnelled there and fifteen hundred people crowded the town and its environs because of its post office, telegraph office, cannery, shops, and boatyards. It remains today a busy place and the site of the Delta's annual Bass Derby.

Walnut Grove and Isleton lie at the very heart of the Delta. The former was founded by ferryman John Sharp (1851) at a key location, the junction of the Sacramento with Georgiana and Tyler sloughs, which give direct access to the San Joaquin via the Mokelumne. Here converged the Indian trails of the old natural levees. They were turned into rough roads. The town got a post office, a militia unit (the Walnut Grove Union Guards), and a sawmill before the end of the Civil War. It really prospered after Steamboat Slough silted up and steamers had to pass its wharf.

Not all of Walnut Grove's great expectations were realized, like that of rafting logs from the Mokelumne through Georgiana Slough to a lumber mill and fruit-box factory. Still, by the end of the decade of the seventies, there were regular stages to Sacramento and ferries to Andrus, Grand, Tyler, and Staten islands. By 1901, bridges were thrown across Georgiana Slough and the Mokelumne. Some say that the bridge across the Sacramento at Walnut Grove, though late (1913), was the first cantilever span west of the Mississippi.

Alex Brown, whose name is almost synonymous with Walnut Grove, was a relative latecomer to the area when compared with, say, Joseph Wise (1853). The New Englander did not reach town till 1879, when forty gambling houses were in operation. He paid them no mind but joined his mother in running the hotel, then opened a general store in 1883. He rented 300 Pearson District acres in 1884, and by 1890, it had grown to 3,830 acres of barley and vegetables, especially beans. Brown was able to raise two barley crops a year, but W. J. Davis warned possible imitators that "labor cannot always be economically used to produce that result."

In his prime, Brown ran not only his ranch, hotel, store, and warehouse, he was agent for Wells, Fargo & Company, Western Union Telegraph, and the Southern Pacific's line of steamers. He was also Assistant Postmaster. Davis observed in 1890, "As can readily be imagined, [he] is very busy indeed. But this list does not quite exhaust the catalogue of his industries."

Brown married Kate Stanford in 1871 and they had five children. When he died in 1923, he was the first citizen of Walnut Grove. His descendants continue such family enterprises as the Bank of Alex Brown.

Walnut Grove is the only Sacramento River town below Red Bluff to occupy both sides of the river. In the 1920s, the Clampett Tract on the right bank, across from "downtown," became an attractive residential section dubbed Asparagus Row, although the pearistocracy was welcome, also.

Behind the levee road of the left bank are modest homes, the old railroad right-of-way, packing sheds and warehouses, and, marked by Ming Mah's barbershop, the remains of old Chinatown. Like Locke, Walnut Grove has been spared by fires, except for the historic hotel, which burned in 1970. Perhaps that is because it employed a *bok bok* man, or night watchman, like Locke.

Courtland was founded circa 1867 by James V. Sims, sometimes confused with Joseph Sims. He was an Illinoian whose only possessions upon his 1852 arrival in Sacramento were the clothes on his frame and a single blanket. But he and his wife, Mary, later prospered. He was a county supervisor from 1871 to 1874, and in 1890 his 120 acres of land were worth $20,000. Sims named the town for his son. The landing got on the map when Capt. Albert Foster enticed the likes of the *Yosemite* and *Chrysopolis* there with a $6,000 wharf in 1871. Shanties of a Chinatown extended the town's limits to the northeast. They burned in 1879, but each reappeared from the ashes, phoenixlike. However, when they were again burned in 1930, landowners refused to grant new leases and most of the Chinese moved to Locke, Walnut Grove, or Isleton. Somnolent now, Courtland prospered in both the Pear and Asparagus rushes.

Hood was a late (1909) railroad town named for William Hood, the construction engineer of the Sacramento Southern. He hoped to build on south to Antioch to connect with the main line, but the spur pooped out at Isleton.

Little remains of Holt, in the South Delta near Stockton, but it was once a humming place with a two-story hotel, speakeasies, bordellos, and a still operating on a barge anchored in a slough. The place-name recalls

Benjamin Holt who, in 1904, invented, nearby, the tractor "that laid its own track."

Isleton was founded in 1874 by a Mexican War veteran, Joseph Poole. He built a drugstore, a smithy, and a harness shop, and served as postmaster. He also provided the landing with a wharf in 1875. A hotel, stores, and a livery stable followed by 1880.

The *Sacramento Union* was "high" on Isleton's prospects because the adjoining land was susceptible to irrigation simply by high tides, which would ensure crops during droughts. Also, the springy peat soil absorbed rain so quickly that "the plowman need not lie idle many hours after the most drenching storm." Crop estimates were eighty bushels of barley per acre, fifty of wheat, and four or five tons of hay—sometimes all from the same field. The paper wrote of Brannan Island, "Anyone who desires to see a nice crop of barley growing on land from which four tons of hay have been taken can have that pleasure by calling on L. Ayer, who will saddle his gallant steed and show him over the island."

Isleton had grandiose dreams when the California Sugar Manufacturing Company arrived in 1876. But the building was abandoned about 1884 and later became a cannery. The town had to wait until after 1900 for the asparagus boom and the slowpoke arrival of the Sacramento Southern Railroad before prosperity came its way. In the 1920s and thirties, three large canneries followed the rails to Isleton and others were built on Bouldin, Andrus, and Grand islands for quick sales of field-fresh "grass" to be canned with none of the usual transit loss. The labor force kept the retail business blocks busy. White families resided in the southern part of town; a Chinatown at the north end became a Mexican barrio after the 1940s. A mile and a half north of town, a suburb of modest homes of farmers, married ranch hands, truck drivers, and others grew up where the road bisecting Andrus Island takes off from the levee road. Isleton last made the headlines in the Andrus Island flood of 1972 when it was swamped and isolated.

Clarksburg, the only town except Rio Vista entirely on the right bank of the lower Sacramento, was named for Judge Robert Clark, a forty-niner. But it did not grow into a Merritt Island "port" until about 1870. It improved when the Holland Land Company took over Reclamation District 999, the Holland District, in 1916. It became a model town in the twenties when 15,000 acres were sold in eighty units for $4,125,000. The buyers were screened, not only for agricultural ability but also for civic responsibility. The arrival of a beet sugar plant kept the village stable, if small. Because of the many Portuguese thereabouts, a Lisbon District adjoins "Holland."

Life in the Delta was typical of small-town America, with social life centered around a close-knit community. The Delta folk have always been ready for fun. Easter Sunday was "proper," but jolly too, with its new duds, particularly bonnets for the ladies. The Fourth of July meant picnics and fireworks balancing speech making by tiresome patriots. The New Year's celebration was followed shortly by the Chinese New Year, enlivened with firecrackers, feasting, a dragon celebration, perhaps a sword swallower, and much of the traditional, ceremonial paying off of old debts with crisp bills in bright red envelopes.

Distinctively local affairs were harvest festivals and the annual June Ball, held in Courtland's Native Sons of the Golden West Hall. This was deliberately an all-night affair because narrow levee roads were dangerous at night to travelers, drunk or sober. The young kids who bedded down in the cloakroom took it as a great lark, or an adventure. Nowadays, local celebrations are Courtland's Pear Fair in July, Rio Vista's Bass Derby in September, the May Festival in Isleton, and Bethel Island's Opening Day parade, bathtub races, and so on, in April for the boating season.

The Delta, early on, became an ethnic potpourri, but hardly the idealized melting pot of sociologists' wishful thinking. For one thing, pre–World War II public schools were segregated there. Japanese, Chinese, and Filipino children attended a grammar school for Asians while, for some bureaucratic reason, blacks and Mexicans were sent to the white school. This unfair treatment still rankles in the memory of Delta Nisei.

Besides the Anglo-Saxon, Irish, Dutch, and Germans, there were Portuguese and Azoreans (Freitas, Dutra, Vieira), Italians (Giavannoni, Picchi), Swiss (Gwerder), Chinese (Lee, Chinn), and Japanese (Narita, Watamura, Sakai). Particularly important and interesting were the Chinese of early days, virtually all of them men who planned, at first, to be sojourners only. They intended to make a pile, then return to wives and children in small villages in Kwangtung to live a life of ease. Many, however, changed their plans. They opted to remain in *Gum Shan*, the Land of Golden Mountains (California), in Delta reclamation and agriculture. Only their bones returned to the old country for reburial according to ancient mores.

The Chinese were subjected to discrimination and some violence by bigoted whites, but they stuck it out with stolidity. Mostly, they worked in gangs led by that rare bird, an English-speaking countryman. He was usually a full-time labor boss, but he could be a local merchant who also made contracts, collected lump sum payments, and divvied up money among field hands. The system was simplicity itself, necessitating little bookkeeping or supervision by the landowners. It was based on mutual trust.

This pool of so-called coolie labor was the only thing that made reclamation possible before the day of modern cost-saving machines like the clamshell dredge. The pay was too low to attract white manual laborers.

Chinese workers sometimes ended up as "voluntary" prisoners of a system of debt servitude. This prohibited upward mobility, socially or economically. Only a handful, at first, picked up a smattering of English, cut off their queues, dressed American-style, and became straw bosses or overseers. Fewer still made it up to the merchant class. When the so-called coolies were exploited, they did not complain—especially if they were "slots," illegal immigrants—because they were innately suspicious of all officialdom.

Until World War I and the Republic of China, few Chinese chose to join the mainstream, whether welcomed or not. They preferred their own people, community, language, food, clothes, and customs. At the same time, barriers were raised against their integration. An 1870 act prevented naturalization of Asian aliens, and from 1882 to 1940, exclusion acts banned further Oriental immigration. Laws of 1913–23 prohibited Asian-Americans from buying or owning land; only three-year (maximum) leases were allowed them. But in 1898 a law case established that American-born children of Chinese parents were American citizens. So the immigrants began to buy land and put it in their children's names.

Life in the Delta was not easy for the Chinese, but compared with nineteenth century Cantonese villages, it was comfortable. Pay was regular and astronomically high by China standards. Truck gardens provided bok choy, pea pods, and other more familiar vegetables; and good fishing—for black bass, salmon, striped bass, sturgeon, catfish, and crawdads (or crayfish)—ensured a varied diet.

There were family and district-of-origin associations, also fraternal and benevolent societies, or tongs. There was the amusement of gambling and the solace of opium at the end of a hard day. (In the evening, a white family's Oriental help, in the lower part of a typical Delta house-on-stilts, might light up and the *ah peen yin* smoke drift up into the living room above.) It is said that special gambling boats also brought pretty sing-song girls up from San Francisco's Chinatown. (This payday tradition was continued in later years by the arrival of bottle-blondes in black Buicks or Cadillacs to entertain the lonely Filipino workmen of ranch bunkhouses.) Chong Chan of Courtland used to give free meals to those of his countrymen who lost their last six bits at the gambling tables.

The vendettas of the *boo how doy,* or hatchet men, of San Francisco's Chinatown tong wars spread to Sacramento but barely brushed the Delta. Its Chinese were split into at least two groups by their Cantonese district dialects, Chung-san and Toy-shan, but the people were peaceful.

When modern dredges reduced the need for manual levee work, the adaptable and hardworking Chinese moved into the stoop labor of harvesting onions and potatoes, where a man would be covered, almost smothered, with peat dust as fine as flour. But they also became skilled in the hand work of pruning, picking, and packing tender pears. Some became family cooks or servants and slowly worked their way up the economic ladder.

The Japanese who arrived after about 1884 differed from the Chinese in being less clannish and more interested in staying permanently and, indeed, joining the mainstream of society. At first, they gravitated to existing Chinatowns, but soon set up their own districts in Walnut Grove and Isleton. There were few Japanese in Courtland, few Japanese or Chinese in Rio Vista. The immigrants from Nippon could not own land after 1913, but Alex Brown who, before he opened his bank, had often loaned money to farmers from his own pocket, leased land to the Issei in an agreement secured by only a handshake.

The heart of a Japanese quarter, the equivalent of a Chinese association hall, was the community bathhouse. It was even more important than the fresh fish market. Like the *temescal* sweat house of the Delta's aborigines that it resembled, it was a social center for relaxation and the exchange of news and gossip after long hours in asparagus fields or pear orchards. A number of Japanese moved up from laborers to bosses and on to the independence of sharecropping by the time of the Delta's World War I agricultural boom.

Isleton's Japantown attracted *sumo* wrestlers who competed for prizes—sacks of rice—after the ring was purified by being sprinkled with salt. There were touring *Kabuki* groups, sometimes local amateurs. During the asparagus season, Japanese women joined Chinese and Filipino women wearing white aprons and caps. They tied up bundles of asparagus with red, blue, or green ribbons to pack crates fresh from the lumberyard. Barbara Brooks Schoenwald remembers still the long-ago mingling of aromas of new wood, fresh-cut vegetables, and the packing of damp moss between layers of "grass." "It was a heavenly smell," she recalls. Finally, colorful labels lithographed in San Francisco were put on the crates to identify each grower. Mr. Brooks's crates bore the Tyler Island Brand and featured his young daughter, with pink cheeks and a big smile under a blonde Dutch bob, holding a bundle of choice asparagus in her arms.

Smells, sounds, and sights of yesteryear mix in recalling the Delta's past. Ms. Schoenwald remembers a kaleidoscopic sensory mix. The smell of sugar beets, incense, fresh fish and bait, sweet Bartlett pear and cherry blossoms, the acrid smoke of firecrackers set off by a fan-tan winner to drive devils away, these are intermingled with the sounds of meadow larks, the three toots of a steamer asking a bridge tender to raise his span, and such sights as slender, elegant Sikhs in turbans—seemingly as tall as the feathered Lombardy poplars of the levees.

In most Delta towns, the buildings were two-story, of frame construction. On the second floor was a store facing on the levee road to trap wharf traffic, often open twenty-four hours a day; on the first floor would be a main street shop below the level of the embankment. In Chinatowns, the second floor was often a residence. Fires wiped out the Chinese quarter of Walnut Grove in 1915 and 1937, and there were blazes in Isleton and Courtland, too, and in Rio Vista in 1892. The Chinese always rebuilt, though Isleton's Oriental district moved from southeast of town to the north end in 1915. Walnut Grove's quarter is mostly a memory, though the old barbershop of Ming Mah survives.

The only all-Chinese town in California, other than such shrimping villages (now ghost towns) as Marin County's China Camp, is Locke. It was born of fire. After the 1915 Walnut Grove blaze, the Japanese rebuilt on the same spot. But the Chinese, under the leadership of merchant Lee Bing (Bing Lee or Charlie Lee Bing), built a new town of their own to the north, on the levee road. They chose the hamlet of Lockeport, founded (1912) by Tin Sin Chan and Wing Chow Owyang when the railroad reached that point. There were only three structures there, one a hotel-boardinghouse for cannery workers and Locke Ranch field hands.

Lee Bing leased land from the estate of George Locke, who had arrived on the Sacramento in 1852. The oral agreement was "notarized" with the customary Delta handshake. Lee, backed by the Yeung Wong tong, built six two-story, $1,200 houses. In its prime, Locke boasted a hotel, bakery, restaurants, barbershop, candy store, saloons, rooming houses, a flour mill, a slaughterhouse, gambling dens, and a Chinese-language school for kids to attend after public school. The peak permanent population may have been four hundred, the seasonal high fifteen thousand. In 1976 there were twenty Chinese families plus some single men. The 1981 estimate was fifty-two residents.

Luckily, Locke was spared by fire, thanks to the *bok bok* man. He was a night watchman who sounded his "All's well!" by knocking a stick against a wooden box every half hour. (The Alex Browns, as well as Chinese merchants, paid a *bok bok* man to look after their Walnut Grove businesses, too. Barbara Brooks Schoenwald remembers, as a child, hearing the reassuring sound of the watchman passing through the yard, opening and closing gates, and the distinctive, clicking "*bok bok*" of his wooden signal. ("It was a comforting sound, for I knew that all was as it should be.")

A Hong Kong businessman in recent years bought Locke for commercial development. Happily, however, the state of California has made it a historical park. It owns the land, but the buildings remain the property of the residents. Besides the old homes, the riverbank warehouse on pilings (now rare), the gardens along the

railroad embankment, there is the grocery store and the decrepit Star Theater, which used to stage Chinese "opera" (dramas) and show Chinese movies, before serving as a rooming house. There is a restaurant, Al's Place, usually called Al the Wop's, named for the late Al Adomi, a bootlegger from Collinsville who bought the building in 1932 from Lee Bing. Al made it locally famous for good booze and steak sandwiches.

An interesting gallery for local painters and craftsmen is the River Road Art Gallery in a building constructed (ca. 1915) by Owyang Tin Git as a drygoods store. In 1928 it became Suen Yook Lim's grocery, pool hall, and ice cream parlor. The Dai Loy Museum of the Sacramento Delta Historical Society occupies the site of an old gambling den, one of Lee Bing's original buildings.

Perhaps the first outside event to have much impact on the isolated Delta was San Francisco's 1906 earthquake and fire. Not only did Deltans ship food and clothing to the devastated city, they took in refugees, including children from burnt-out Chinatown.

But it took World War I to really jolt the Delta out of its sleepy rural isolation. Most farmers were draft exempt, for agriculture was critical to the war effort and subsequent European relief programs. Liberty and Victory bonds were purchased, to the eventual dismay of Deltans who learned that Herbert Hoover then spent the money raised buying beans—in Japan. Delta farmers wholeheartedly responded to government urgings and went on a binge of overproduction, especially in beans and grains. They sold off their draft animals to the Army, and horses and mules never returned in great numbers because of Ben Holt's invention of the tractor, near Stockton.

World War I profits could not stop the postwar agricultural decline which bottomed out in the Depression of the 1930s. Eleven bond-issuing reclamation districts defaulted. (All recovered eventually, thanks to another war, but restricted their activities to levee and ditch maintenance.) The farmers' faith in the Bank of Alex Brown kept it solvent, but other institutions, like the Bank of Courtland, went belly-up in the thirties.

Even as expert a farm family as the Van Loben Sels clan was badly hit by the Depression. P.J. came to the U.S. in 1876 to see the Centennial Exposition, but ended up in San Francisco, where a banker financing reclamation had him replace the man in charge. When Van Loben Sels could not convince the banker that much more money was needed, he went home to the Netherlands, raised a bundle, and bought the land himself in 1892, 3,700 acres for $130,000. But the family, which had had to start all over again after the 1907 flood and was still paying off its debts, lost the Pearson District property once more in the thirties. They showed their typical Delta spunk by starting fresh for a third time, buying some land and sharecropping other fields.

Hobo camps appeared in the 1930s, one smack on the tip of Andrus Island in full view of Walnut Grove. The down-and-out would beg for food. Many would just "borrow" vegetables from fields for their aromatic stews. One enterprising fellow rowed entirely around Grand Island, stopping at every farmhouse for a handout until he and his buddy had laid in enough of a larder to tide them over the winter months.

The canneries in the Delta all died because of the recession and because the railroads and good highways made centralized packing in the cities more cost efficient as the Delta labor force dwindled. Young Japanese and Chinese were moving to the cities. Today, only a few old packing sheds remain on individual farms for boxing fresh Bartletts for fast shipment direct to markets.

The Delta's economic illness continued right up to the much-too-drastic cure of World War II. But the Eighteenth Amendment at least flattened the decline between 1918 and Repeal in 1933. Liquor—or rather, Prohibition—created a new, if illegal and underground, industry—bootlegging. The Ryde Hotel became the most popular "blind pig," or speakeasy. Thomas H. Williams founded the hamlet of Ryde and named it for his hometown on the Isle of Wight. At its peak, it boasted only two canneries, a few homes, a landing, a post office, a general store, and a hotel. The basement "speak" was raided several times and finally it and its secret tunnel and still were closed down. Today, it is a thriving roadhouse restaurant and bar.

Rarely were rumrunners caught in the Delta during Prohibition. Sympathy was with them, not with the revenuers. But in February of 1928 the constable of tiny Birds Landing led a posse in a tule crawl in Montezuma Slough to seize the *Hawk* and its cargo of 113 sacks of Scotch (twenty or thirty bottles per sack), 17 of champagne, and 16 of gin from three armed crewmen who, fortunately, did not resist.

Prostitutes in the Delta in the thirties were both white and Chinese, often brightly dressed girls who were kind to children. One Chinese matron recalls that she was first treated to Jello, when she was a little girl, by one of the Caucasian "nymphs." Locke was a wide-open gambling town, but Walnut Grove's Bank of Alex Brown handed out much more silver to its citizens than to Locke's. A carpenter claimed to have made more money as a dealer for three or four hours an evening than for a full eight-hour day of honest toil. Gambling dens had watchful doorkeepers who sounded the alarm if lawmen grouped outside for a raid.

Steamboating faded fast in the depressed 1930s. River freighting gave way to trucking, and passenger traffic yielded to privately owned Model A's. The California Transportation Company "went under" in 1930. The surviving firms consolidated as The River Lines and kept the Sacramento River's overnight "superliners," *Delta King* and *Delta Queen*, running till World War II. ("Floating bagnios," their critics called them.) Their hulls were built on the Clyde in Scotland, but they were finished in 1926 in Stockton. On their beam ends, financially, they went into war service and never returned to the Delta. The *Delta Queen* is now a popular cruise ship on the Ohio and Mississippi rivers, her sister-ship a half-sunken hulk at a Richmond shipyard, still awaiting financing and restoration to make her a floating restaurant on San Francisco's Embarcadero.

The Issei and Nisei who were evacuated to camps in World War II were replaced by Filipino and Mexican workers. Many Japanese-Americans did not return. Isleton's were unable to pay off their indebtedness between the 1927 fire and the 1942 evacuation, so they did not come back. Walnut Grove's *Nihonjin* were luckier; Alex Brown's family honored its commitments and took care of their homes, mostly paid off, until their return.

Basically, the Delta has remained a prosperous and stable place since the roller coaster economics of World Wars I and II. This is because many of the children and grandchildren of pioneer settlers have chosen to remain there, with a stake in the area's future, and because some who left as young people are beginning to return. Newcomers, who fall in love with the area, have helped, too. For all of the large-scale, corporate development, especially in the South Delta, a sort of rural gentry has survived from the Kerchevals, Runyons, and others. But it is really upper middle class, not upper crust. This well-educated and highly motivated community has deep roots. They practice modern farming techniques, which insure both high production and soil conservation, while preserving regional traditions.

The post–World War II books of Erle Stanley Gardner, Bob Walters, and Hal Schell have converted thousands of Californians into confirmed Deltaphiles, or "river rats." Powerboaters, yachtsmen, houseboaters, and water-skiers have joined the anglers who have been in the Delta since the days of the Pescadero Indians. Though there has been a loss of water quality from boating pollution, aquatic sports and recreation have worked beautifully alongside agriculture. Bethel Island is the curiously frenetic heart of boating in this tranquil land of contentment. But the most charming places are lonely, cozy, little "gunkholes" where a few boats can raft up in the tulescapes of Snodgrass Slough,

The Meadows, and Lost Slough, the area Gardner called The Everglades of the West. There are twenty Delta-based yacht clubs and other boating organizations today.

The decline in water quality has hurt sport fishing, though anglers still come to the Delta in schools to cast for stripers or plug for black bass, from Rio Vista to Franks Tract. Duck hunters still huddle in the dawn's cold in skiffs or blinds out in Suisun Marsh, though reclamation has reduced California's marshlands from 5,000,000 to 400,000 acres.

The whole state can be thankful that the Delta has remained in the hands of pioneering families with a strong respect for the land and its natural and human history. So far, they have kept this fragile agricultural heartland safe from the "progressives" who have flooded Hetch Hetchy, silted and fouled San Francisco Bay, and ruined Owens Valley and Mono Lake. But absentee speculators and "developers"—this time wheeling and dealing in water rather than land—have fixed their chilling gaze on the Delta.

The Central Valley Project opened the door a crack. The California Water Plan grew and grew, not like Topsy but like Dr. Frankenstein's monster. Shasta Dam first regulated river flow, then the Cross Delta Channel shunted some of it to the San Joaquin Valley, via pumping plants in Tracy, and over the Tehachapi Mountains to the Los Angeles Basin. Even this modest amount of siphoning has increased the incursion of salt water and raised the temperature of the fresh water enough to cause water hyacinths to proliferate into great masses of floating vegetation that jam boat propellors and clog channels, sloughs, pumps, and conduit intakes, and literally block pleasure craft from marinas.

Comparing the problem of hyacinths with the looming threat of the Peripheral Canal is like matching a mosquito bite against a gunshot wound. Should the voters of California approve Senate Bill 200 in June, 1982, a forty-three-mile-long swath, four hundred feet wide—the size of a thirty-two lane freeway—will be cut through prime land. It will divert up to 70 percent of the Sacramento's water at Hood, before it gets to the Delta, and send it southward up the San Joaquin Valley. Supporters of the project admit that it involves a billion dollar "dig." Critics estimate that the added energy costs of boosting the water over the Tehachapis will run the tab up to twenty-three billion dollars.

Already Southern California voters are being wooed. Soon a media blitz will tell them that cheap and needed water will be coming their way, for a pittance. They have not been told, of course, that Los Angeles already has a surplus of water. That the city not only "dumps" water, but resells its supply to agriculture—which already drinks up 86 percent of California's supply. Naturally, the Southern California taxpayers are not told that they, unwittingly, are subsidizing the dirt-cheap rates of water for big agribusiness. Should the Peripheral Canal be built, most of the water will not go to flats in Santa Monica or bungalows in Pasadena, but to enormous fields in Kern County where multinational conglomerate agribusiness grows cotton to export to the Orient.

Opponents, like State Assemblyman Tom Bates, who have studied the Peripheral Canal plan, predict the following results: first, it will destroy hunting and fishing, then it will poison the area. The Delta will revert to a swamp, but this time to a salt marsh. Its lazy sloughs will become too toxic even for tough "channel cats." Worse will be the domino effect on shallow San Francisco Bay: with the rivers' flushing action taken away, the bay, even with its tidal action, could become stagnant and polluted.

And, of course, the rich heritage of the Delta would then be lost—the legends and lore of such places as Trapper Slough, Beaver Point, and Whiskey Slough, Dead Horse Island, Prisoner's Point, and Lost and Disappointment sloughs.

This would be a heavy price to pay. Such cheaply irrigated, superproductive soils as the Delta's should remain in food production forever, with controlled aquatic recreation as a happy by-product. For the ultimate price may well be not just the Delta itself, and San Francisco Bay, but the destruction of California's key ecosystem.

The sheer luck of its relative remoteness has spared the Delta, so far. But its protection has also been a shared responsibility of its immediate guardians (its local settlers) and local, state, and federal governments. Miraculously, it remains today a pastoral landscape that would delight a poet like William Wordsworth, a painter like John Constable. As a long-time Delta resident puts it, "Its openness makes your soul expand."

Artists, historians, and other writers have neglected the quiet Delta for more obviously dramatic scenes—the Mother Lode, the High Sierra. Only a few novelists have even touched upon the area—Wallace Irwin, Joan Didion, Leonard Gardner, and Maxine Hong Kingston. Ansel Adams chose to photograph the Sierra, Alma Lavenson the Mother Lode. Edward Weston skipped the Delta in his hurried *Guggenheimjahr* of wandering. But Pirkle Jones, Roger Minick, and Steve Simmons have lately trained their lenses on the scenic and historic Delta. Simmons is, in his way, almost as close a student of the region as Dr. John Thompson, himself. His photographs, which extend this narrative, serve as a visualization of what all Americans have to lose if we sacrifice the Delta, this region of great historic, scenic, and even spiritual values.

Facing: Spring storm, Grand Island

Abandoned railroad bridge, Snodgrass Slough

116

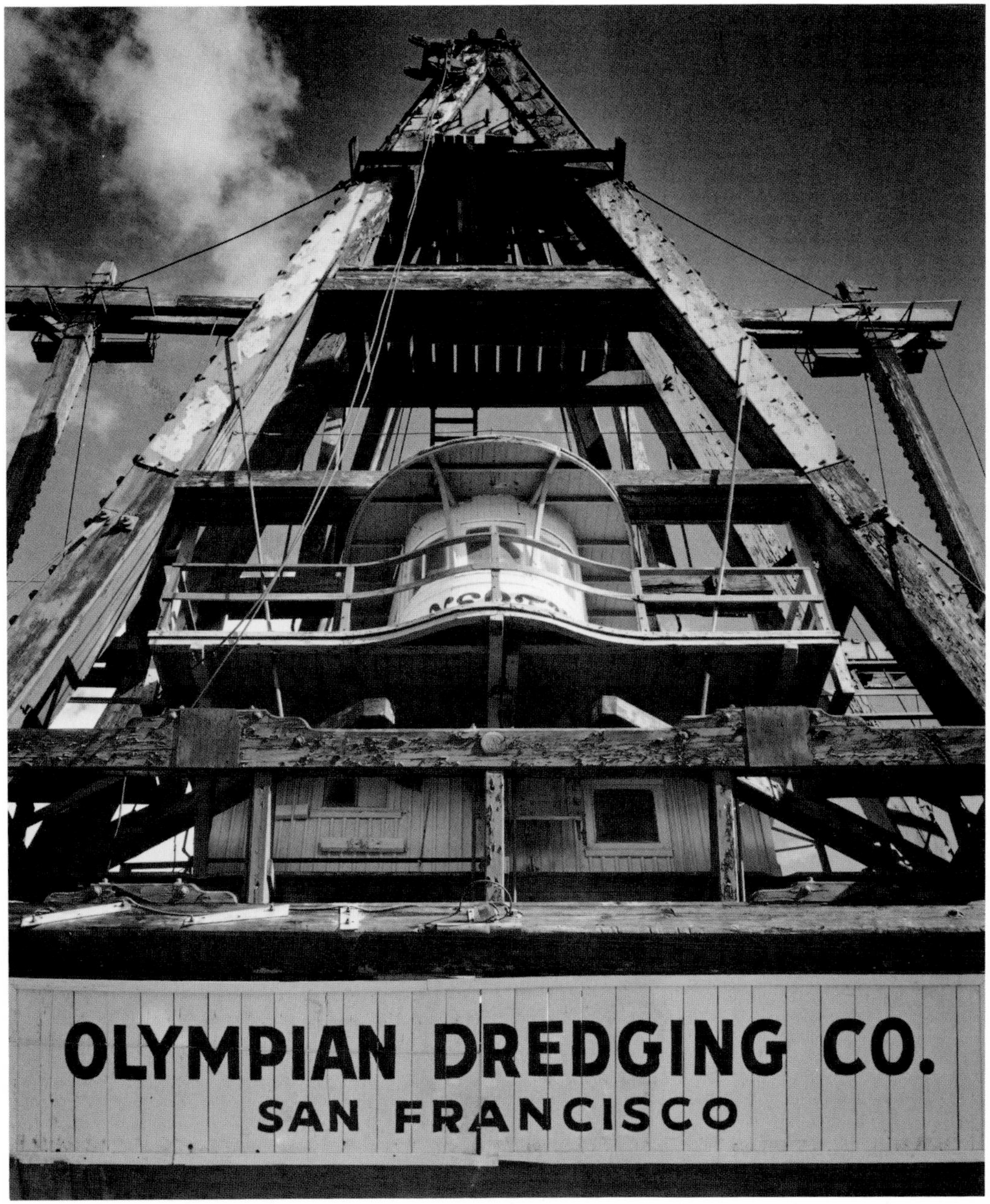
OLYMPIAN DREDGING CO.
SAN FRANCISCO

The Neptune

Japanese section, Walnut Grove

Japanese bathhouse, Walnut Grove

Old storefront, Japanese section, Walnut Grove

Main Street, Locke

121

Chinese Association Hall, Isleton

George Greene home

Dennis Leary home

Front porch, the Miller place
Overleaf: The Meadows

MY TASK IN THIS BOOK HAS BEEN TO SHOW you the Delta as it is today—the stately old mansions that recall a life of elegance, the not-so-grand towns that have a pride and dignity all their own, and the rich but delicate land that proved to be the most difficult to photograph. I have grown to love this small part of California—broad and open, yet so fragile. It is important for us to hold onto a place such as this. It is our heritage, our sense of past, and provides us with a grounding from which we can move forward.

Most of the images for *Delta Country* were made with a Calumet 8x10 view camera. The exceptions on pages 45, 54, 118, 119, and 120 were made with a Galvin 2¼x3¼ view camera. Lenses used ranged from one-half to two times normal, and the selection depended on the available working space and the desired interpretation. Film for the 8x10 was Super-XX, and Extapan was used in the Galvin. All film was tray developed in a Metol and Pyrogallol film developer.

The images for this book were made between October 1978 and November 1981, with the majority of the photographs selected for the book made in the last eighteen months. The combination of an increased familiarity with the area and the switch to the 8x10 in late 1979 seemed to open up a whole new world for me. Knowledge, feeling, and vision are all skills that take time to work into close collaboration. Some of the images were carefully planned as to the best time of year, angle of view, and weather conditions, while others were stumbled onto fortuitously. The view of Mt. Diablo on page 24 took over a year to find just the

Photographer's Note

right combination, while the views on pages 15 and 43 reached out and selected me one afternoon as I drove along some of the levee roads.

My growth as a photographer has been carefully nurtured by several people in the last few years. My first note of thanks must go to Jim Galvin, who has either built, repaired, or modified most of the camera equipment I've used in the last five years. Additionally I would like to thank Gordon Hutchings and Ralph Talbert who have critiqued my work and offered me continued encouragement to keep up my efforts to produce the elusive but successful image. But beyond their practical help, their willingness to lend a sympathetic ear has been greatly appreciated. I must also acknowledge the contribution made by Morley Baer. My brief contacts with him over the last few years have given me a tremendous appreciation for his imagery and provided me with an added enthusiasm to pursue my own work. Dewitt Bishop always seemed to be there with an old wooden tripod or other piece of oddball equipment that always was exactly what I needed. And finally a note of thanks to Alan Ross who shared his many years of darkroom experience and offered valuable advice while I was making the reproduction prints for the book.

As I spent time wandering the Delta's levee roads, I had the opportunity to meet a group of long-time Delta residents who richened my experience immeasurably. To Lenore (Greene) Allen, Clyde and Edna Bishop (posthumously), Bessie and Gee Chinn, Herman Fisher, Bob Jang, Roland Lauritzen, Dennis Leary, Roberta Lee, Christopher Lee, Dick and Marie Phipps, Clarence Pratt, Toshio Sakai, Grace Scribner, George Smith, Carel van LobenSels (posthumously), and June Watamura I extend my deepest appreciation for our leisurely conversations in which they shared their memories of life along the Sacramento River.

And last, but certainly not least, I want to thank Bill Chleboun. Bill learned early on of my interest in doing this project and helped me hold it together until it was completed. Without his help my work may have been finished, but never published.

Steve Simmons

Sacramento, California
November 1981

Bohakel, Charles A. *The Historic Delta Country.* Antioch, Ca., author, 1979.

Bohakel, Charles A. *The Indians of Contra Costa County.* Amarillo, Texas. P & H Publishers, n.d.

Bohn, David and Minick, Roger. *Delta West.* Berkeley, Scrimshaw Press, 1972.

Brewer, William H. *Up and Down California In 1860–1864.* Berkeley, University of California, 1974.

Bryant, Edwin. *What I Saw in California.* Palo Alto, Lewis Osborne, 1967.

California Resources and Possibilities. San Francisco, California Development Board, 1920.

California Today. San Francisco, California Promotion Committee, 1903.

Carson, James H. *Recollections of the California Mines.* Oakland, Biobooks, 1950.

Chapman, Charles E. *California, the Spanish Period.* New York, Macmillan, 1939.

Cook, Sherburne F. "The Epidemic of 1830–33 in California and Oregon." *University of California Publications in American Archaeology and Ethnology.* Vol. 43, No. 3. Berkeley, University of California, 1955.

Cook, Sherburne F. "Expeditions to the Interior of California; Central Valley, 1820–1840." *Anthropological Records.* Vol. 20, No. 5, Berkeley, University of California, 1932.

Cutter, Donald C. *The Diary of Ensign Gabriel Moraga's Expedition of Discovery in the Sacramento Valley,* 1808. Los Angeles, Glen Dawson, 1957.

Cutter, Donald C. *Spanish Exploration of California's Central Valley.* Berkeley, University of California (unpublished Ph.D. dissertation), 1950.

Dana, Julian. *The Sacramento, River of Gold.* New York, Farrar and Rinehart, 1939.

Davis, William Heath. *Seventy-five Years in California.* San Francisco, John Howell, 1929.

Davis, Winfield J. *An Illustrated History of Sacramento County . . .* Chicago, Lewis Publishing Co., 1890.

Dillon, Richard H. *Fool's Gold.* Santa Cruz, Ca., Western Tanager, 1981.

Dillon, Richard H. *Great Expectations: The Story of Benicia, Ca.* Benicia, Heritage Book, Inc., 1980.

Dillon, Richard H. *Siskiyou Trail.* New York, McGraw Hill, 1975.

Dutra, Edward. *History of Sidedrift Clamshell Dredging in California.* Rio Vista, Dutra Dredging Co., 1980.

Ellison, William H. *The Life and Adventures of George Nidever.* Berkeley, University of California, 1937.

Gilbert, Frank T. *History of San Joaquin County, California.* Oakland, Thompson & West, 1879.

Gilliam, Harold. *San Francisco Bay.* Garden City, N.Y., Doubleday, 1957

Grimshaw, William R. *Grimshaw's narrative . . . ,* edited by J. R. K. Kantor. Sacramento, Sacramento Book Collectors' Club, 1964.

Hodges, R. E. and Wickson, E. J. *Farming in California.* San Francisco, Californians Inc., 1923.

Irwin, William H. *Augusta Bixler Farms,* Brookdale, Ca., author, 1973.

Killingsworth, W. G. *Deciduous Fruit Growing in California,* San Francisco, Californians, Inc., 1923.

Lantis, David, *et al. California, Land of Contrasts.* Belmont, Wadsworth Publishing Co., 1963

Leale, John. *Recollections of a Tule Sailor.* San Francisco, George Fields, 1939.

MacMullen, Jerry. *Paddlewheel Days in California.* Stanford University Press, 1939.

Selected Bibliography

McGowan, Joseph. *History of the Sacramento Valley.* New York, Lewis Publishing Co., 1961.

Phelps, William D. *Fore and Aft.* Boston, Nichols & Hall, 1870.

Sacramento, The Heart of California. (Sacramento, 1914?)

Schell, Hal. *Dawdling on the Delta.* Stockton, Schell Books, 1979.

Schenck, William E. and Dawson, J. "Archaeology of the Northern San Joaquin Valley." *University of California Publications in Archaeology and Ethnology.* Vol. 25, No. 4, Berkeley, University of California, 1929.

Schenck, William E. "Historic Aboriginal Groups of the California Delta Region." *University of California Publications in American Archaeology and Ethnology.* Vol. 23, No. 2. Berkeley, University of California, 1926.

Shine, Steven M. *Early Years to Golden Years in Rio Vista.* Vallejo, Ca., Victoria Books, 1978.

Shine, Steven M. *The History of Birds Landing, Ca.* Concord, Ca., Victoria Books, 1976.

Stories of the Sacramento River Delta. Rio Vista, *Delta Herald and River News,* 1952.

Taylor, Bayard. *El Dorado.* Palo Alto, Lewis Osborne, 1968.

Thompson, John. *The Settlement Geography of the Sacramento–San Joaquin Delta.* Stanford University (unpublished Ph.D. dissertation) 1957.

Tinkham, George V. *History of San Joaquin County, Ca.,* Los Angeles, Historic Record Co., 1923.

Wells, A. J. *California For the Settler.* San Francisco, Southern Pacific (Passenger Department), 1910?

Wilbur, Marguerite E. *A Pioneer at Sutter's Fort.* Los Angeles, Calafia Society, 1941.

Wilson, Edward. *The Golden Land.* Boston, J. E. Farwell, 1852.

(Wright, George F.), ed. *History of Sacramento County . . .* Oakland, Thompson & West, 1880.

Yates, John. *A Sailor's Sketch of the Sacramento Valley in 1842.* Edited by Ferol Egan. Berkeley, Friends of the Bancroft Library, 1971.

Index